Now that I have
lighted houses, wha...

- display by Linda Olsen / Millie's Hallmark

More...
Village Display Tips

A compilation of creative ideas and tips
to enhance your village displays
from collectors for collectors

Published by

Leigh Gieringer Graphic Services
Scottsdale, Arizona 85251-1257

Copyright: © 2005
Published by:
Leigh Gieringer Graphic Services
7150 East Camelback Road, Suite 444
Scottsdale, Arizona 85251-1257

ISBN 0-9664775-4-5
Printed in the United States of America.
First Edition: 2005

Library of Congress Number: 98-093227

The purpose of this book is to educate and provide ideas to collectors of lighted villages to further enhance their enjoyment in displaying their collections. Ideas and photographs have been presented
from numerous collectors throughout the United States and so cred-
ited. Any photo not otherwise identified was provided by Leigh
Gieringer. The author and publisher shall have neither liability nor
responsibility to any person or entity with respect to implementation
of these ideas.

*This publication is not affiliated with Department 56®, Inc. or any of
its affiliates, subsidiaries, distributors or representatives. Department
56®, Inc., The Original Snow Village, The Heritage Village Collection,
The Dickens' Village Series, The New England Village Series, and The
Christmas in the City Series* are Trademarks of *Department 56®, Inc.*
Eden Prairie, Minnesota. *The Alpine Village Series, The North Pole
Series, The Little Town of Bethlehem Series* and *Snowbabies* are the
copyright of *Department 56®, Inc. The Disney Village Series* was a
joint venture by both the *Walt Disney Company®,* and *Department
56®, Inc.* Product names and product designs are the property of
Department 56®, Inc.
    The photographs contained herein were submitted by village
collectors. The lighted buildings and accessories incorporated in the
photos were used solely to illustrate display ideas, techniques and
tips. *Leigh Gieringer Graphic Services* is not affiliated with any company whose products may appear in this book.

FROM TOP: Ed Logan, Bernie Dvorak, Debra Blue and Linda Olsen

FORWARD

As collectors, one of the aspects we like most about collecting lighted houses is the fact that the latest introductions often bring new design ideas, new technologies, and most of all ... new opportunities. These new opportunities I speak about center around creating displays.

Years ago, Christmas in the City collectors, for instance, never dreamed of needing to create water scenes—other than, perhaps, a small pond in a park. But today, bridges span rivers and bays while boats head to shore. At one time, North Pole fans thought that all they needed to do was have snow everywhere with a few hills thrown in for diversity. Now they use items related to the licensed products. And, over the years, Dickens' Village has gone from a small town feeling to a city with a sprawling Victorian city with suburbs, complete with rivers and yes, even items designed to sit along the sea.

For many years now, displays — large or small, intricate or simple — have been a major part of collecting villages. Even in the earliest years, collectors put together scenes, although they were almost always very basic. All it took was a little cotton batting here, a few evergreen trees there, a few houses, and a lot of imagination, and a perfectly fine village display sat on a mantel or under a tree.

Today, however, displays, like most things in life, have changed. Some collectors use their God-given talents and continuously fashion small, highly detailed scenes throughout their homes. Others build large, sprawling cities and towns that, once finished, stay in place for months, if not for a year or more. Still others enjoy the buildings with little or no frills surrounding them. All of these, and everything in between, is perfect.

This book is here to help you develop and implement your ideas and those of others. No matter what style display you wish to create, in the following pages are suggestions and techniques that you will not only find useful, but ones that will also spur other ideas that may otherwise have never occurred to you.

These techniques come from collectors like yourself. Many of the concepts are original, while others have been passed on by fellow collectors. Of course, others are a combination of several skills. Some you will be able to duplicate, and others may lead you to other conclusions. But, all are here to get your creative juices flowing and to assist you in making the display you have always dreamed of or the one you thought never possible.

Be sure to look at each idea collectors have offered. If it's not shown in your village, yet you like it, try it anyway. You may just surprise yourself. After all, it's your village, and as long as you enjoy creating your display and getting satisfaction from your results, that's all that matters.

Happy collecting, and happy displaying!

Peter George, Publisher
Greenbook Guide to Department 56 Villages

Several new sub-series have been issued recently. It makes it easy for newer collectors to acquire a complete set. Walt Disney Showcase and SANTA Anniversary pieces are shown above as part of a larger display. Or, they can be used in small vignettes.

For collectors of miniature porcelain villages, one of the most exciting times of the year is when new pieces are introduced into your favorite village. One can day dream for hours thinking about what pieces will be added into an existing collection, how they will fit into it, and if there is some special way that those buildings can be showcased, treated or placed to make them truly awesome. Sometimes, the search is on for small accents - or display techniques - that will make that building or set of buildings standout in a vignette, or as part of a larger display. Perhaps the question is which buildings will go with what. It matters if space is limited, or if the display follows a theme. Other times, a building is so personally attractive that it just has to come home, even if it doesn't go with the others in a collection. Can it become a part of an eclectic display, or should it take center stage as a special vignette? It is hoped that this display reference will help both those who are new to collecting, providing them with step-by-step instructions to setting up a display; and those more seasoned. After all, numerous heads are better than one, to provide new and different ways to enhance a village display. *More Village Display Tips* is packed with stimulating ideas.

- display/Leigh Gieringer/Millie's Hallmark

$\mathscr{C}$ontents

- *display by Debborah Whitson*

So many collectors focus on creating miniature villages with mountains and waterfronts. There is also another way! And, the pieces look great all year long. Include some of them in your home decor. Find related items that blend in terms of theme and color, and connect them together with flowing accents such as these grapevines and fish netting.

Debborah Whitson (Arizona) has the imagination to find suitable items in antique stores, craft stores, thrift stores and elsewhere. She also possesses the magic touch to create artistic and dramatic settings on just about any horizontal surface. Another of her displays can be found on page 100 and the rest of this one on page 113.

AN OVERVIEW
To Develop Great Displays

$\mathcal{E}$very collector is different. Some may just have received their first piece and haven't a clue what to do with it. Others may have almost the complete Snow or Dickens' village and have been creating dynamic displays for thirty plus years. Then, there are those who started collecting just recently, got the bug and now have a hundred or so pieces; or maybe inherited a village or two and are not certain how to proceed. Any of these sound familiar?

Of course, there are also those who found a few buildings they like or received one as a gift. Sub-series grouping like the Victorian Christmas, All Hallow's Eve, the Ballparks, Mickey's Christmas *(top right)* or the Snow Village Valentine's or Easter buildings make the choices easy since they are designed as stand-alone sets.

The *Original Village Display Tips* and *Volume II* both have numerous ideas submitted by collectors. *More Village Display Tips* continues to offer new ideas and techniques for collectors of all ability levels. Based primarily on pieces issued after *Volume II* was released, this book provides ideas and techniques not contained in the other two.

For those just starting out or want a refresher course, there are simple to follow ideas to develop a quick set-up using styrofoam. ***Sandi Moore*** *(top left)* has many ideas to help one get organized and develop a dramatic display. We are also very privileged to have **Bernie Dvorak** *(middle left)* showcase the development of a display containing mountains, water and a desert. And, ***JD Robb*** *(bottom left)* shows us how to create realistic mountains using Geodesic Foam. Both Bernie and JD conduct seminars at Collector Gatherings. For those who cannot attend these Gatherings, *More Village Display Tips* brings these experts to you.

I've tried to include ideas applicable to all villages. Many are very versatile, such as creating background mountains and developing different ways to indicate water. They can be included in any village whether it is a winter village or non-snow. Other techniques work best with one village or one piece within a single village. An example is camouflaging the blue bases found in select pieces. They look unnatural just set in a display. *(middle right)*

Vignettes *(bottom right)* are the perfect way to enjoy one or more pieces whether they are only up for a short while, or if they are to be enjoyed year around. Or, dedicate a space and change it periodically throughout the year. And, they don't have to be placed in the traditional sense - with complementary scenery. In fact, use your imagination. Select your favorite pieces and place them as accents to form an eclectic setting as part of your room decor as was done on the proceeding spread.

There is a cornucopia of ideas submitted by several collectors. Some are basic and others are more advanced, thus there should be something new for everybody. Credit is given to those who contributed content, displays and /or provided photographs of their display. If a display has no credit information, it was created by or photographed by yours truly.

Parts of three Dickens' sub-series are included above. The beauty of these smaller villages within a village is that they can be made into a mini display under the Christmas tree - or wherever - as a set like A Christmas Carol, Hallow's Eve, or Queens Port. They are all inclusive or can be included into a large display as above.

THE INTRODUCTION OF SUB-SERIES WITHIN A VILLAGE CAN ENCOURAGE SMALLER DISPLAYS...

Years ago, collectors tried to acquire every building within their village or villages. Like trees - one could never have too many buildings! However, there have been a tremendous amount of buildings introduced in the past several years for most villages. Many long-time collectors have run out of space, so they have become more selective with their purchases.

One of the things attracting newer collectors is the intricate designs of recent buildings. Many don't have the desire, time or finances to obtain a complete village the size of Dickens', CIC, North Pole or even New England, much less Snow Village. Thus, in recent years,

there have been several village sub-series brought to market. The advantage is that newer collectors have the opportunity to acquire a complete, coordinated village. Typically limited to ten or less pieces, the display is workable for easy set up and dismantling. If one desires to add more, they can always find several other pieces which will fit architecturally and increase the size to make a very pleasant and controlled setting. Or, these smaller villages can become districts within a much larger village if their owners have been collecting awhile.

Because of the limited size, a compact, but detailed display accommodating the pieces can be built of styrofoam, wood, or other building material(s) - some of which are described in later chapters. Once completed, it can be brought out every year. Minor adjustments or new sections can be added, but for the most part, putting it up each year will not take a lot of new effort. Numerous techniques revealed later in this book can be used to develop some special settings.

...OR, EFFECTIVELY EXPAND IT WITH DUPLICATION.

Line up the roof tops of several Dickens' Row Houses. Alone, the building gets lost, but together, they attract a lot of attention.

IF ONE IS GOOD, TWO OR THREE MAY BE BETTER

As one looks at a large display from a distance, most single buildings blend into all the others unless there is something distinctive about it. It might be its size, shape or coloration - or a combination of all

these design elements. When you see such a building, it just stands out, like St. Paul's Cathedral or a windmill. Thus, if you want to emphasize a less distinctive building, you have to create something to make it more noticeable.

Another good example of duplicating a piece is the Victorian styled apartment buildings which could double as high-end office buildings. The viewer would definitely spot these within a large display. Because this is a store display; all the Ball Parks facades are lined up as background features. Since they have a consistent depth, they make excellent three dimensional backgrounds. Placed in the far back, detailing is diminished, thus building identification names and a lot of the other details become less significant. LeMax has come out with a bunch of facades. Facades provide an interesting alternative to styrofoam and trees, and don't take up much room. Use a variety of backgrounds.

One way is duplication. They become much more visible. Of course, most buildings would look silly if there were more than one unless there is a logical reason. Excellent examples include the

Who could resist this hub of activity: To bring attention to an area, create a lot of interest around it. Detailed areas grab the eye, especially if there are other "relief" areas which are open - snow fields, unoccupied park terrain or vertical mountain escarpments. Some areas should be busy: Other areas left simple.
- display and photo by Rose Heidcamp

Dickens' Row Houses and CIC Apartments. After all, the citizenry has to live some place and grouping several of these buildings together is logical and can create an impact.

Other ways to highlight special buildings have been covered in the other books. However, by isolating a building, it will bring attention to it. You can do this by elevating it, placing it on an interesting platform, putting white space around it, highly detailing the nearby area or adding special effects to it.

MIX ITEMS INTENDED FOR ONE VILLAGE INTO ANOTHER

The red and green ice cubes are typically thought to accent a North Pole scene. But, look at the effect they have on the Snow Village Diner. Find little things like these colorful cubes and picture them surrounding your favorite Christmas buildings. If an item is attractive to you, you can always find an application for its use in one of your settings. Purists don't follow this philosophy, but look at items suggested for other villages and mix them with yours. Or, pick up suitable miniatures from doll stores, craft stores or discount stores. Don't limit yourself. Items from other sources personalize your village. It makes for a more interesting and unique display.

Other good mixes to consider could be the following. Some are covered in greater detail in subsequent chapters.

■ Borrowing Dickens' Village pieces for Alpine. The Alpine castle is very whimsical. Use the Windsor Castle in a distant mountain elevation. Stump Hill Gatehouse would look appropriate with the earlier Alpine pieces. *(page 50)*

■ Church facades such as Westminster and Notre Dame can be stand alone vignettes, but both could be merged into a CIC display.

■ Several pieces from different villages can be put into themed displays. A water theme comes to mind with the Queens Port (DV) pieces, East Harbor (CIC) and water related New England pieces.

The red and red cubes have a dramatic effect when added to your favorite pieces - even if it isn't North Pole. - display by Linda Olsen / Millie's Hallmark Snow Village

The latter are smaller pieces, so they would look best in the background. Fill the foreground with a lot of detail so the attention stays in the front, while the background pieces become atmosphere. *(page 68)*

■ Some New England pieces can be reconstructed into Old England. The Blacksmith shop design blends well with buildings such as the Mustard shop or Christmas Carol buildings. In exchange, the Clock and Watches can be rebuilt next to the NE Bank. The colors, architecture and size effectively relate.

■ Other really good matches include DV Gas Works and Notting Hill Water Tower. Both have distinctive shapes, they are painted in

coordinating colors and they are very impressive as a set. Everyone has their favorite buildings, but when setting up a display, look for the ones that go together as well as the aforementioned duo. The subseries' referred to earlier are designed to work together in terms of style, color, size and architecture. The village designer should be able look at the buildings he/she has, then form the composition with a keen eye to which buildings complement each other.

■ Carnivals are always fun, either as a stand alone display, or as a part of Snow Village, CIC or Disney. The animation and strong red coloration make these a main focal point of any display. Create a

Many of the North Pole pieces have accents in purple and yellow-green tones. Gather those together so they are in close proximity; then separate them with another building in traditional colors to break up the color palette. Note the middle building has little purple, but it does have the yellow green - enough to tie the buildings together without the purple dominating the scene. An expansion of this scene was seen on page iv. The purple tones are picked up again several buildings to the left.

Battery run bright LED lights can be inserted into any building which has a standard cord.

larger midway with stands made by LeMax or make your own game booths from balsawood. Tiny Teddy Bear "prizes" are available in many colors. Use paint tones that accent the Ball Toss accessory. Depending on how many you make, some can carry the bright red. Color some in gold. For others, match the strong blues and other tones featured in the Carousel or Tea Cup pieces. Make signs on a computer. A couple of souvenir shops can be borrowed from the Ball Parks. Or, make your own souvenir carts/stands from wood or resin pieces available in other lines. Gather mini's to add to the carts. The hunt and construction is half the fun. Some of the ideas offered to increase the size of the Ball Parks also work with an amusement park scene. Also see ideas on page 88.

Several newer buildings are battery operated. The idea was a good one so special pieces can be included in table top centerpieces. The biggest problem is that they are not very bright, especially compared to a building that is connected to a cord and a seven watt bulb. ***Bob Herman*** *(Arizona)* has made a battery operated LED light. He makes them in different color combinations for various effects. Placed in any porcelain building which uses the standard cord, they are just as bright as a normal bulb. The battery is placed under a "snowdrift" made of Plaster of Paris which can be conveniently placed next to the building in plain sight. Thus, there are no cords to trip over or hide.

The following chapters have many more ideas to add to your next display. Try some of them!

2
STYROFOAM
For Quick or More Advanced Display Building Solutions

*T*is seven days before Christmas and all through the house, there are several people stirring, since the villages are not up yet! Sorry, it doesn't rhyme, but you get the picture. We've all been there. What is needed is a plan to get a village created in a very short period of time and still have it be impressive. This is how **Sandi Moore** *(California)* handled her quick display. Being organized helps tremendously. She and her husband built this one in an afternoon.

ELFLAND IN THE PM

An 8' by 14" table was built out of wood for stability during the previously week. It was attached 40" above the floor, against the wall where the sofa usually sits. However, the sofa was not removed from the room. It was placed a couple of inches in front of the finished display table so the grandchildren can kneel on the seat cushions to view the village. A couple of other tables lined the wall to accommodate the overflow.

All the items to be used were removed from their boxes and organized on tables - buildings in one section; porcelain accessories in another area. Trees and shrubs were gathered together. And, fences, light poles, walkways, and other miscellaneous accents were grouped for easy access.

In this display, the table top was covered with a one inch thick piece of high density

Remove the buildings and large accessory pieces from their boxes and place them on a convenient table. It also helps to group them by color, size and/or function for quicker selection. A final placement should consider balance of these design elements. Having all the red roofed buildings together is as detrimental to the display as having all the larger buildings at one end and the smaller ones at the other.

- display and photos by Sandi Moore

(blue) foam. To save time, most of the elevations were eliminated, although they do not take a great deal of time to add, if more are desired.

THE ORGANIZING PROCESS

*"How do you decide where to place each piece? This is the most important step in setting up a display: The buildings and large accessories determine the 'feel' of each area within the display."**

Sandi started on the lower section. Daylight beams from the window, while at night, a curio cabinet light helps illuminates this area. This section contained many of the unlit pieces and outdoor activities.

The Wedding Chapel should be elevated, so that was placed on a hill in the back with the icy pond bridge

connecting it to the surrounding area. Grouped nearby are the school and children related activities such as the Petting Zoo and Pony Ride, plus the Spa. The Candy Cane Shack and Hot Chocolate accessories fit into this section, too.

The elevations, in this display, were created using stacked boxes, books and scraps of styrofoam. Sandi makes a rough sketch of the building positions, removes them temporarily, then builds up the layers with construction materials until the desired height has been reached. Cotton batting is used to represent the look of snow drifts.

The next grouping is comprised of Grandma's Bakery and other food related buildings, plus as a convenience to "Grandma" - and the other

*Quote: Sandi Moore

Separate the porcelain accessories (TOP), trees/shrubs (MID) and other accessories (LOWER) from the other pieces so they can be found quickly when needed.

Most porcelain accessories come in sets of two or more. Keep those pieces together in pre-set up and if possible, when they are placed into the display. If you are in a hurry to box them soon after the Holidays are over, they become easier to find and the display takes less time to disassemble.

This same principle works for all villages especially for small to mid sized displays. For a real large one, work in sections, do the back and hard to reach areas first. Determine which buildings fit into each section and organize them into their respective groupings. Stack them in separate sections of the room and keep the items boxed until you are ready to work with that section.

However, items like trees, fences, street lights, benches, walkways and other pieces that are universal and can be used anywhere should be grouped together in set-up. Thus, all will be readily available and can be selected as desired to complete each scene. For the non-purist, it is also advisable to gather other appropriate items including materials to lay under buildings, develop courtyards to unify and bring additional interest into the display.

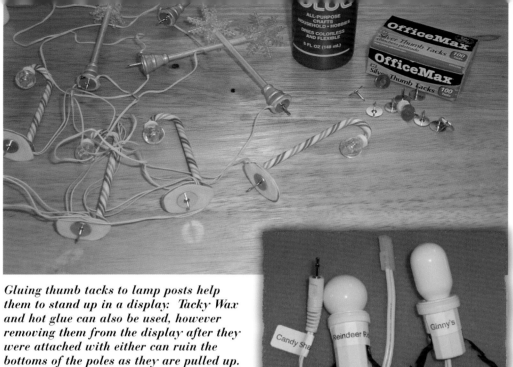

Gluing thumb tacks to lamp posts help them to stand up in a display. Tacky Wax and hot glue can also be used, however removing them from the display after they were attached with either can ruin the bottoms of the poles as they are pulled up. Additionally, they will need to be attached to a clean surface. Thus, adding a thumb tack is best for temporary displays, since the thumb tack can remain on the bottom when stored.

Many of the newer cords have additional wires protruding from them. To prevent them from getting mixed up, label them, as well as the adapters that go with them. Again, this is a time saver in both set-up and break-down. No wasted time in locating and testing the proper cords.

Since many of the new buildings have their own adapters, use electric strips made for computers that allow for plugging in several at a time. Otherwise, the adapters cover up needed outlets.

ladies in the village - the Beauty Shoppe, the shoemaker and the clinic are located in close proximity. Look at the type of building. It is easier to organize when the functionality of each building is determined and they are placed near similar types of businesses.

PUT BACKGROUNDS IN PLACE

The background in this display was made using Foam Core™. This material, available at art and craft stores, as well as office supply centers, consists of a piece of foam sandwiched between two pieces of two-ply cardboard. It comes in a variety of different colors, including blues for skies and black for a

Halloween night. If you will be covering it with fabric, use white.

Cut the Foam Core to fit the wall area needing to be covered. Sandi used two 20"x30" boards cut into four 30"x10" pieces, and taped them together to form a 120"x10" background. Select an appropriate piece of fabric. After the Holidays, fabric stores often have deep discounts on seasonal fabrics. Thus, if

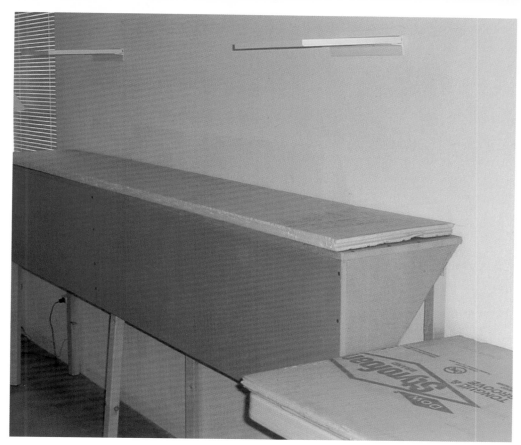

A sturdy 8' by 14" table was fabricated from plywood and pressboard. Legs were added to bring the height to 40" above the floor - a good height for viewing the details of the display. It was secured to the wall with brackets. This type of base is especially good for permanent displays. High density styrofoam was used as a display base. Two other tables were added for the overflow. The shelves above provide extra display areas. Make certain there are electrical outlets nearby. Have several electrical strips available.

As an easy to obtain alternative for temporary displays, there are 2'x4' card tables available at most "Big Box" stores which can be folded and conveniently stored. However, they are more expensive and not as sturdy. Once covered with a suitable fabric attached to the face, the empty boxes can be stored out of sight under the display.

you can't find any at special prices before the Holidays, pick some up for next year's displays in January. Utilized solid colors, too.

In this display, three and a half yards of fabric featuring snowflakes with silvery sparkles on a deep blue background were used. Attach one edge of the fabric to the back of the foamboard. Sandi used two-inch clear shipping tape to adhere the fabric to the board. Two-sided Scotch Tape or velcro can also be used. Hold the Foam Core in place and attach it onto the wall with several small nails. Tuck the sides of the fabric under the board against the wall and let the remaining fabric fall behind the table. The background is nailed about 18" above the table, so 8" or so of background doesn't have a board behind it. If the fabric is not

PLACEMENT IS PERSONAL
PREFERENCE, BUT GUIDELINES APPLY

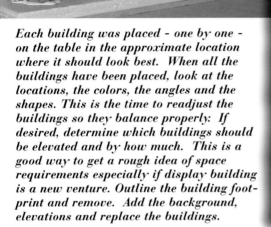

Each building was placed - one by one - on the table in the approximate location where it should look best. When all the buildings have been placed, look at the locations, the colors, the angles and the shapes. This is the time to readjust the buildings so they balance properly. If desired, determine which buildings should be elevated and by how much. This is a good way to get a rough idea of space requirements especially if display building is a new venture. Outline the building footprint and remove. Add the background, elevations and replace the buildings.

cut to fit the background, it can be removed from the Foam Core, cleaned, folded and reused next year even if the display has different dimensions. When the display comes down, a little spackling compound can fill the holes left by the nails.

DETERMINE THE PLACE-MENT OF BUILDINGS AND LARGE ACCESSORIES

With the background in place, the next step is laying out the buildings. Many of the larger accessories pieces take up a lot of room, so place them into position at this time, too.

*Elevations make a display more realistic and interesting. Styrofoam comes in various thicknesses including 2", 1-1/2", 1" and 1/2". Use them all to obtain a rolling landscape. (See page 50.) Each can be stacked to increase the height and make it easier to view the buildings in the back. Several pieces of styrofoam can be secured together with **Low Temp** Hot Glue or Barbeque Skewers. The benefit of using skewers is speed and that the base can be taken apart easily. If the glue is too hot, the styrofoam will melt and not adhere to the other pieces.*

FROM TOP TO
BOTTOM: Secure
the background in
place, then run the
light cords along the
back of the display:
Multi-bulb strands,
Place'n Plug™ cords
and strings of
miniature lights can
substitute for the
individual cord that
comes with the
building as long as
it is standard issue.

Florist pins are
ideal to attach thin
styrofoam scraps to
the base. They can
also secure the elec-
tric cords in place.

Sandi uses cotton
batting to cover the
cords and soften the
edges of the boxes
and books she used
to create her eleva-
tions.

A very large
piece of white mate-
rial represents the
snow. Once the base
is prepared, build-
ings, ground cover,
walkways, lights
and accessories are
added.

Once the buildings are placed, insert the light into the piece. Add the elements in the back first, such as the larger trees seen above. Then work forward with street lights, walkways and other accessories toward the front.

Determine where any special features such as ponds, streams, court-yards, etc. should be placed and mark these area(s). Many quick displays will not contain these elements unless they are the stock pieces available from one of the manufac-turers. These features can also be created throughout the year in one's spare time, and brought out to be included into the display.

The quick way to elevate is grab anything with varying height such as boxes and books, then cover with Blanket of Snow or some other white fabric as shown on the previous page. Holes for the light bulbs can be cut through the fabric so cords are buried under the fabric. How-ever, when fabric or batting is used, sometimes the accessories with small bases don't stand up as well as on the harder styrofoam. And, since white styrofoam is available in numerous thicknesses from home improvement stores, the material makes very nat-ural rolling hills, can be carved into craggy rocks and cliffs, and can also be painted, if desired. All of these required more effort. Thus, if time is

ABOVE: The finished display lines one entire wall and took a half a day to build once the table was constructed and anchored in place.

BOTTOM PHOTOS- PREVIOUS PAGE: Details of the display show the lamp posts pinned into place, the tree groupings and the multi-colored sidewalk pieces unite the top section. The white "snow" is a white knit fleece found at a fabric store, and draped over the entire display. Because it easily stretches, it works well to contour a varied landscape between the buildings. Cut holes in the fabric to allow the light bulb and socket through. The cords remain under the fabric and are thus buried.

Different walkways are added in different sections, uniting them to the buildings in that area. Pick a style that matches nearby buildings. For instance, the red, green and white vinyl road looks best under buildings which are designed with the traditional North Pole red or green roofs and architectural coloration.

Curving walkways and buildings make the display much more interesting than laying them out straight. The background fabric adds atmosphere and ties the display together.

critical, keep it simple!

Many newer collectors have the tendency to line the buildings in a row, so all the front doors can be seen at a glance. That's perfectly normal, after all, go down most city streets, and the majority of doors are parallel to the curb, the distance between the buildings is uniformly spaced, the building footprints are approximately the same distance from the street, and most buildings have similar elevations. That's city planning 101 created by the engineering mind. Left brained people -

artsy, creative types - look at the world differently. Streets are curved. Buildings reside at different elevations. Some are closer to the streets. Some are set back. Some are angled. Some are grouped together. And, some should stand alone. There is no Home Owner's Association to limit the imagination or flow. A building may have a great looking side or back. If it looks good at another angle, showcase it! Don't let a bulldozer level the landscape. Vary the height, angles and coloration.

THE SEVEN
SANTA BUILDINGS

A SANTA'S: Literally the most plausible, but the display would look ridiculous if the two "S" buildings were separated so one was in the second position and the other on the far end. AS SANTA: (Shown above) balances much better. The center towered buildings become the focal point due to their size, position and prominence, and the left hand "A" somewhat offsets the grouping of four buildings to the right. Styrofoam is positioned prior to shaping. It is easier to visualize the layout when the buildings are put into place.

The center section is shown on the preceding page. It is carved with the Hot Wire Foam Factory Free-Hand Routing Tool out of a block of 8" thick packing styrofoam to look like an iceberg. The section to the left was placed on its side so it would not be as high as the center section. Stacked sheets of 2" styrofoam pieces are placed on the right. Smaller pieces were added to create the levels. All were set on 1" styrofoam bases so the "water" line was the same for all sections. - display and photos by Leigh Gieringer

This display uses the 15th Anniversary Santa pieces. However, this version of SANTA has seven letters. There are two "S"s and three "A"s. The S and first A buildings are duplicated, with different coloration. But, if the building angles are changed, and one is elevated, they look like two wings of the same building. Business is booming, thus Santa needs more room to make all those toys for good little boys and girls, and train his staff of elves.

The center section was created first as a stand-alone vignette, as seen on the cover. The eight inch thick styrofoam packing chunk was rescued from a trash bin. What's that old adage? *One man's trash is another man's treasure!*

With a hot wire, carve the edges and the bottom, leaving enough sty-

It's any collector's prerogative to change one's mind! S-SA-ANTA seems to be the best solution to the seven building SANTA neighborhood. The reason: The similarly shaped "A" buildings are different enough so that they look very good together as a set. The sign on the newer building makes it the choice to place toward the front. With the angles and elevations varying, and the colors coordinating, the pair makes an attractive duo. It is much stronger scene than separating them. The area which opened up will be easy to fill with accessories, or if this is a part of a larger display, place another building there.

rofoam to have the piece set solidly on a piece of 1" styrofoam. Deep crevices were intensionally carved into the styrofoam "iceberg" to represent fissures in the ice. A set of 35 blue miniature lights was placed in back of and under the "berg" and secured with Florist's Pins. Set aside.

Pale Aqua, French Blue and White paints were sponged onto the piece of 1" styrofoam. In this example, no primer was used. When the color is still wet, the tones were encouraged to merge. Dab the colors on until satisfied. Areas under the berg can be painted darker since they will be in shadow. Darker hues exaggerate the shadows. Let it dry thoroughly.

EnviroTex Lite®, the two-bottle system, was used here. Woodland Scenics has an easier resin called Realistic Water™. If you are very careful and not pour too much resin on the styrofoam, you can control

Finding materials to place under the buildings - especially in North Pole - is fun. So many different covering are available. TOP: Paper liners from some restaurants are available in red, black and blue, probably more colors. The scale is perfect. LOWER: Scrapbook papers offer variety for all villages. Scrapbook paper is more durable. Both can be cut and shaped as desired. Or, use multiple sheets to unite more than one building.

Taupe colored linoleum squares were shaped to form the foundation of the two "S" buildings. Although several other more colorful coverings were tested, I choose six-sided ceramic tiles (available in 12" square sheets at a home improvement center) because the color blended with the linoleum. They are easy - translation: fast - to work with; and, they are a neutral color to unite the entire set of buildings. If this was part of a larger display, which it very well could be, the choice of ground cover will tie these buildings together as a unit, yet not be boring. Additionally, strong colors are native to this village. I wanted the attention drawn to the buildings and other added details, not on the ground cover. When other buildings are added, some will be set on strong colored tiles, papers, various stone-patterned linoleum squares, marble squares and other surfaces for variety. In this display, I also wished to subdue the tones so the blue lighting reflecting on the sea and in the crevices would stand out.

Sheets of stone or brick patterned plastic can be painted to fit the scene. Found at model railroad stores, sheets can be cut, curved, or used in multiples. Another example appears on page 58.

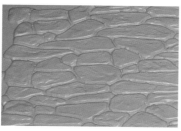

A clear plastic tree sits on a battery run Fiber Optic base which changes color.

The overall display is approximately 6' by 2'. White and red plastic; and white feather picks represent trees, along with white sisle trees from JoAnn's Santa's Workshop line. The simple backdrop is styrofoam panels with the blue film protector left attached. Detached film is crumpled and draped in select areas to provide a shadowed effect.

the seepage. Be advised that this can make a real destructive mess if the resin spills over the sides. Put plastic, or another protective covering over your work area for protection. Wear latex gloves to protect your hands. Don't get it on clothes.

Pour a small amount in the center. With the back of a plastic spoon, draw the resin over the styrofoam you want covered. Repeat until the entire piece is covered in a _very thin_ coat - about $1/32$" Bring the resin up to the edges with the back of the spoon. Let it set. Time will depend on temperature and humidity. This iceberg was placed on the ocean while it was still wet, thus it is permanently attached. Although the lights do not touch the resin, they cannot be removed from this scene.

The other modular sections were created. The one on the left was created in a similar fashion. The one of the right was merely carved.

Icebergs, like islands, do not have to match up. The top surfaces are connected with bridges. The water level is connected with loose carved pieces of styrofoam ice, stretched cotton surf and swimming seals. The right section has white plastic "trees" to hide the split.

Neutral toned linoleum pieces were shaped to form a platform for both S buildings, while the rest sit on six-sided ceramic tiles. These come in 12"x12" sheets and can easily be broken apart to form the desired shape under and around the pieces.

Unlike most resin, porcelain or sisle trees, picks don't take up much room. Because they are thin, they can go just about anywhere and soften the look of the display. Periodically, many picks are available at discounted prices. The white picks are perfect in this setting. With stems included, these picks measured almost two feet long. The branches were cut off and strategically placed in the display. These three picks provided about 25 individual trees. The red ones added color and the small feather picks provide a soft, willowy look.

Another string of blue lights was pinned to the back of all three pieces. Styrofoam mountain peaks provide a backdrop behind the taller buildings, while the rest sit in front of styrofoam panels with the blue backing retained.

A crumpled sheet of backing was pinned to the panel - the shadows provide a small amount of shading seen when a distant object is viewed. The easy blue background also serves to accent the white icebergs and the buildings set upon them. Accessories complete the picture.

Since the Arctic Trees retired, there have been slim pickings for those who appreciate totally white trees. These fir trees were found this year, but they only come in one size. For formal settings they can be placed in rows along fences, in parks or town squares; or symmetrically in front of select buildings.

GOOD WHITE TREES ARE DIFFICULT TO FIND

If you like the whimsical look there are plenty of trees for North Pole, but what if the cutesy look does not appeal to you. When you think of the North Pole or a scene at higher elevations applicable for most of the other villages, trees are draped with thick layers of pristine, white snow. Green trees - even green trees tipped with a small amount of white - don't look very natural here.

Occasionally, white sisle trees can be found. These, found at a fabric store, only come in one size. It's up to the display builder to create different elevations for the trees to sit upon. *See the pictures in the next column.* Take the bases off. They look more natural when the wire stems stick directly into the styrofoam. Remember, they look best in odd number groupings.

However, for most settings, adjustments must be made, since trees look more natural when they are different sizes. Therefore, build up the styrofoam layers beneath them so there is a noticeable height difference. D56 makes place setting card holders which were converted into a clothes line for Santa's suit. Look in the scrapbook section for tiny detailing additions like Santa's outfit, and mitten sets. The moose in the background are metal silhouettes from a craft store.

PICK A TREE OR SEVERAL TREE PICKS
FOR ACCENTS, FILLERS & TO HIDE THE CORDS

If you have collected villages for a long time, you probably have some favorite trees that have been discontinued. Although there is still a variety of trees available through manufacturers, the selection is limited and for the most part, they are bulky. They can be grouped, but take up a lot of space. Because of size and detailing, they are best used as special accents. If there are styles that you find work well for you, get a lot of them. They will be discontinued and your village will probably grow. That, of course,

LEFT: Numerous pick styles can be used with any winter scene. The appearances change from year to year, so get plenty when you find a style you like. RIGHT: There are picks for every season. These are right off the shelf, but don't forget that a can of black spray paint can alter them to fit a Halloween scene. Or, add additional canned snow.

means you will need more trees to surround the new buildings.

Like nature, a well designed display will have many different "species" of trees. Due to the quantity needed, evergreen picks are a great addition. In the past several years, the green and white ones are not the only ones available. Crystal clear, blue, and silver ones can effectively be

A variety of resin trees can be found at hobby stores, craft stores and some discount stores. They are very versatile. Because they are inexpensive, they can be sprayed with black for Halloween, or cover them in white paint for Alpine, North Pole or any snowy mountain top

The imagination can run wild in creating a North Pole village. Red picks brighten the layout and make a design statement. Blue adds a cool appearance. The clear makes it look very cold. Mix and match a variety of picks. Balance the colors against the buildings and other accents. Refer to the display on pages 30-31.

scene in Snow Village or New England. Or, leave them green and group them around the display. The brown stone fence with patches of accent snow can also be covered entirely with white paint for the North Pole. If desired, allow some of the brown to show through.

added to most winter scene displays. The proceeding, plus red and gold picks can be absolutely striking in a North Pole village. Those with glitter are particularly effective with colored lights focused on them and reflecting surrounding color off of them.

Picks are inexpensive and lately have come in several lengths. When on sale, they are only pennies, thus very affordable to get in quantity. They can be placed as backgrounds and around buildings to soften the hard corners. Several picks can hide the cords between building groupings, as well as areas leading to the buildings. Place the picks in groups with the stems close together. For a taller groupings, use the longer ones in the center and combine a bunch of similarly styled picks around them to create a larger tree or a grove of trees. Because they are mostly two dimensional, they can be put at different angles to look thicker.

TOP: Pine trees are easily made with a Scroll Table and 2" styrofoam scraps. With a pencil, outline the shape, or design the shape as you cut the styrofoam. The only restriction is that they cannot be higher than the wire. When the shape is cut out, sliver it into four or five clones. It speeds up the process! MID: When displaying, turn some 180° so they look different. They are especially appropriate for a high mountain scene and NP. BOTTOM: Make several different sizes and shapes and line the back of the display. Highlight with lights for special effects.

MAKE YOUR OWN TREES OUT OF STYROFOAM

It is a quick process. They are light weight and add interesting design features to a winter setting. If desired, colored lights can be placed between a solid background piece and the tree silhouettes to emphasize the contours. This treatment was used in the *Creating Large Display* DVD with purple caps on a string of miniature white lights. The caps provide more subtle, softer hues. Use the colored lights if stronger color is desired. The best part: they are cheap!

The process can also be used to create eerie Halloween tree silhouettes. Painted black, and back lit, they are a striking addition to Hallow's Eve and Halloween villages. Strings of miniature orange or purple lights - similar to Christmas lights - are available in craft stores for the fall season.

EXPANDING AN EXISTING DISPLAY

Parts of the display on the next page may look familiar. The right side was featured in the *Creating Large Displays* DVD. The left side was added after the video was completed. The challenge was two-fold: to make it fit into the style and motif of the existing displays, and find the room to expand. The best way to duplicate the style is to replicate the display elements found in nearby scenes. In this case, glass blocks, styrofoam igloo bricks carved in an identical style, blue lights and the Nutcracker accents were repeated. And, the a fairly wide hallway became a narrow path.

As a temporary display, the bases are make-shift. . . pressboards over small tables and boxes. . . basically odds and ends found in the garage. The display was built around several pieces of furniture, sections of which were allowed to become part of the display. The tall tree becomes a focal point, hid the edge of the older section and helped unite the two sections.

Several 8'x4"x2" styrofoam strips, available in home improvement centers, were cut into two sizes: 12"x4"x2" and 8"x4"x2". A hot knife was used to carve the front surfaces, duplicating the design element carried throughout the other display sections. They were placed like ice bricks of an igloo to curve around the boxes.

The 2004 North Pole intros other than Elfland were placed in this section. The front and foremost positioning of the pastel colored buildings brings attention to them. They are surrounded by the traditional red and green buildings. The entire section, as seen on the next two pages, has animation scattered throughout since these are the newer pieces. The older pieces have a different look, thus are concentrated in another display on the other side of the room. *(Refer to the Creating Large Displays video.)*

Extending an existing display
is easy if the design elements are
duplicated. The styrofoam blocks
are carved in a similar fashion.
Similar lighting techniques were
used. And, the addition of the Nut-
crackers and colorful gift
boxes - many in reds and
greens help to unify the
old and the new.

- displays and photos by Leigh Gieringer

MODULAR DISPLAY BASES ADD IMPACT: THEY CAN BE DESIGNED TO BE USED INDIVIDUALLY OR IN GROUPS

Display bases can be made for any village, a special piece or several selected pieces. Place the base within a large display. The viewer's eye will automatically be attracted to it. Or, use it in a vignette such as the Elfland display on this page. This one consists of three modular bases that were added together in combination. They can also be used individually. They were designed for an entirely different set of buildings, thus these are versatile.

Even in a vignette, the borders of the base can be expanded merely by placing a building outside the wood bases. In this case, a small piece of white Foam Core board was cut in a multi-angular shape with uneven edges and dusted with "Real Plastic Snow". The angles were determined by several factors: the table it was set upon, the shape of the building which was to set on it, and the position of the staircase in the display base.

These custom bases are hand-made by **Bob Herman** (Arizona) The lighter gray ones - pictured, go with most villages, but the bases can be made in other colors in tones of gray or taupe. Or, they can be colored with white paint mixed with glitter for the North Pole. A little black paint and some distressing and they will fit into a special Halloween setting, too.

To determine the shape of the bases, a footprint of each building which was intended to be set on them, was provided. The design was drawn to complement the pieces.

The elevated part of the platforms provide places for larger buildings, while the walk-way below can hold street lamps, café tables, small buildings and other accessories. These lights are dark, but wires from a lighted set can be placed under the accessory bases and hidden under the snow. Don't tape the wires down. Tape may pull off the paint. It is difficult to see in the picture, but the walls separating the two sections, as well as the front contour are curved. They make a wonderful addition to any display.

Porcelain animals were added to expand the horse population in the Pony Ride piece. If the shiny appearance is bothersome, spray the horses with a matte or dull coating available at craft stores. Thin pieces of styrofoam were used to raise some buildings on the top level.

If you saw this amount of detail in a large display, do you think it would get notice? You bet! As previously stated, detailing draws attention to a building or an area. Do you think you can have too much detail? Nah! It will keep viewers coming back to see what they missed before.

No matter what the village, many buildings suggest a theme. Work with that theme and let the imagination go. Here are a couple of examples. The first features the Teddy Bear Training School which was created by **John and Pat Ehrenreich** *(Maryland)*. The smaller photo shows the entire basket display.

The detailing is incredible, little bears attending classes, sitting at computers, listening to Ms. Professor Claus and receiving their diplomas. They are learning how to act after they're adopted! Benches and screens were hand-made. The base-

- display by John & Pat Ehrenreich

ment room is lit. An etching tool was used to create the cobblestones and igloo blocks. Even the background mountains sport outlines of teddy bears. Information on how those were done can be found on page 73.

Many of the Crayola® accessories found here are Christmas tree ornaments. Others are hair barrettes or other children's jewelry: - display by Pat Murray

One of the reasons why so much detailing is possible for North Pole is that the companies that license D56 to create a building with their name on it, also license other products. The important factor is to find items that are size compatible. ***Patricia Murray (Arizona)*** found a plethora of Crayola® merchandise which added much interest to her North Pole village.

Hair barrettes were taken apart and uniformly hot glued to a couple of painted balsawood sticks. Most of the larger items are Christmas ornaments carrying the Cray-

ola® theme. The Lego® building, sharing this courtyard, is another piece which lends itself to serious fun. In addition to walkways, fences, bridges, city squares, trestles and tunnels built from Lego® blocks around the building, multi-level platforms can provide display space under the structure. The space could be used for train tracks, streams, walkways or an underground mall for vendors or even Elfland since the buildings are small. Check the Lego® website to buy the blocks in bulk by color. Other logo buildings offer many interesting possibilities

FROM DESERT TO SEA,
to Historic London Town:
Tell the Stories of the Past

Some of the most interesting displays are based on actual historic times, events or places. It's a beautiful way to teach others the story behind the display. In this chapter, there are several magnificent displays. The first explores the Little Town of Bethlehem Village which has peaked a lot of interest. Contrary to some opinions, the old and new can be blended effectively. **Bernie Dvorak**, *(et. al.)* from Maryland put a grand effort into this awesome display, not only in its creation, but also in his instructive narrative. This is how he, and his team, put this exquisite display together.

THE LITTLE TOWN OF BETHLEHEM

For the first time in recorded history, the entire world is at peace! The Roman Empire extends into the land of Israel. A decree has gone out from Caesar Augustus that all men are to register for the census in the city of their birth. Thus, we arrive at the focal point of this display:

Located 2,500 feet above sea level, you can now visit the walled city of Bethlehem, where the Christ Child was born. Fishermen haul in their nets on the Sea of Galilee. Caravans approach from the desert. Angels trumpet the birth of a newborn king...

... *"For unto us a child is born, Alleluia!"*

This Little Town of Bethlehem is a stunning and beautifully built display:

- display and photos by Bernie Dvorak and team

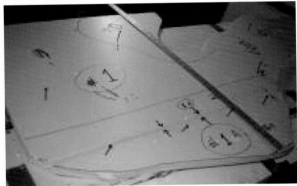

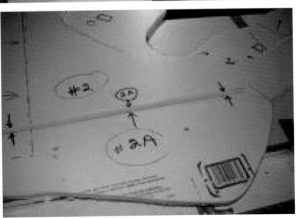

This display features three elements: mountain, desert and sea. The mountain is made of three 2" X 2' X 8' sheets of styrofoam and 2½ pounds of paper maché. The mountain rests on a base composed of three pieces of 1" X 2' X 8' styrofoam which is also used to form the desert and the sea.

THE BASE & MOUNTAIN
54"L X 32"W X 16"H (8 - 2" layers)

We begin by securely duck taping a 1" X 2' X 8' piece of styrofoam to a 6' folding work table.   Next, we will use a sharpie to draw the rough shapes, that will form the mountain, onto a 2" X 2' X 8' piece of styrofoam. Layer #1 *(left)* is 54" long and 32" at the widest point. It will look something like a fishhook. Use the other end of this sheet to form #1A into a triangle. This will complete layer #1.

Draw layer #2 onto the second sheet of 2" Styrofoam. #2A is also a separate triangle.

Layer #3 goes on the last 2" styrofoam sheet. #3A is also a triangle. Note that these are photos of my one inch patterns. Your styrofoam will be two inches thick.

The rest of the mountain can be as high as you like. I used layer #4, #5, #6, #7, and #8 all shaped to form the elongated letter "C" in progressively smaller sizes. The top layer on this one

TOP TWO: Level one - two perspectives. BOTTOM TWO: Level two - two perspectives. Draw the shapes with a sharpie and remove unwanted styrofoam. Use the cutaway pieces to extend the level - straight edge against straight edge. Blue and pink styrofoam is denser than white, resulting in finer detailing possibilities.

is 25 inches long at the peak. That makes the mountain 16" tall with a base of 2" for a total display height of 18." You will have enough scraps to cut out these pieces with some left over.

Cutting styrofoam is simple. Almost any tool that works on wood, will also work on styrofoam. I use an inexpensive Black& Decker® jig saw, with a wood cutting blade, to cut out all of these pieces. The hot knife cuts, but it also seals styrofoam. That is precisely what we do not want to do on this model. We want it rough, in order to make a home for the paper maché, which we will apply later.

The back is intensionally left rough.

Now cut out all of the parts and stack them in order. (RIGHT TOP) Place your LTOB lighted pieces on your mountain, as you want to display them. Allow room for streets, and cut out areas that are too tight Cut holes for the power cords large enough for the plugs to easily fit through.

Do not spend much time at this point trying to shape the mountain. Look at the photo of the unfinished back of the mountain. It is very irregular. It is these irregularities that will make the finished project look lifelike. Now put your village pieces away.

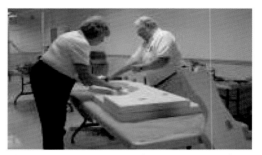

Cut out the parts and place them in order.

Form the mountain to desired height.

The mountain is shaped with a wire brush.

Apply the paper maché with a putty knife as if you were icing a cake. Start at the bottom. Concentrate on vertical surfaces.

At this time, it is very important to thoroughly vacuum all sides of the styrofoam pieces that you have cut out. Tiny pieces will interfere with the gluing process.

We will now begin our ascent up the mountain. *(Refer to pictures on the previous pages.)*

First fasten #1 and #1A pieces to the board that we taped to the worktable. Use 2" sheet rock screws, at a straight up and down vertical angle. These "temporary screws" hold the project in place, freeing both hands for wire brushing later. The straight up angle of the screws will allow you to pull the mountain straight up off of the bottom piece and easily remove the screws, when the mountain is complete.

Next, paint the bottoms of #2 and #2A with white glue such as Elmer's. Use it full strength. Align them on top of #1 and #1A. Now press down and screw them in place using about eight 3" sheet rock screws. This time you must insert the screws on a 30 to 45 degree angle. This locks the platforms solidly in place. Use the same procedure on level #3. Continue this process until you reach the top.

Now, we are ready to shape our mountain. You can do it all by hand with a wire brush. The old rusty brushes are the best, since they are firmer then the newer wire ones that are available today. I like to start at the top of the mountain by removing the sharp corners of each layer by alternating between a side to side, an up and down, and also some diagonal strokes. You can also use a drill with a circular wire brush attached in order to save time, as

I do in my seminars. However, you will still use the manual wire brush to finish preparing the surface for the paper maché. Remember, we are doing two things with the wire brush. We are shaping the mountain, but more importantly, we are creating cavities for the paper maché to cling to. The rougher the surface, the better!

Have you ever baked a cake? I know you have ladies, but I am talking to the guys out there! What we are going to do now is put the icing on the cake. *Gentlemen: ask your wives to help you with this.* In fact, get the whole family involved. Here is how we begin.

Cover your nose and mouth with a paper mask and pour about three pounds of paper maché into a plastic container. Add one cup of white glue for each pound of maché. Add four cups of warm water to the container and mix thoroughly. Continue adding water, 1/2 cup at a time, until you reach the consistency of cake icing. When this mixture is right, a putty knife placed in it, will be able to stand up on it's own.

With a putty knife, begin icing the cake from the bottom to the top. For the most part, we will only do the vertical surfaces.

Paper maché is recycled newspaper that has been cleaned, dried, and ground to a fine powder. Dry glue is added. I don't trust the glue content for display projects, therefore I add one cup of white glue for every pound of maché. "Celuclay ™" is the brand name of the product that we used. It is widely available. A one-half inch coat will dry outside, on a warm 75+ degree sunny day, in about 12 hours, depending on the

water content. It will become rock-like in its hardness, maintain it's lightweight characteristics, and last indefinitely. It can be sawed, drilled, and painted. Wet leftovers can be placed in a plastic bag and stored in the refrigerator for several months.

Back to the mountain. Begin at the bottom and apply the maché to about a three inch high by two foot strip. The desired thickness should be between a half inch and one inch. Return to where you began and use a palette knife - or similar type - and cut the surface with random diagonal, horizontal and short vertical strokes. Make the incisions as deep as possible without exposing the styrofoam. This must be done before the material begins to "set-up", usually within 10-15 minutes.

Go to the next "row" above the one you just completed and repeat the procedure. However, this time, make your slashes extend into the strip below the one on which you are working. Don't be afraid to make long (2" or 3") slashes, side by side, going down into the previous section. This will destroy any hint that it was done in row sections. That is very important for a natural look! Work your way around the mountain. I recommend starting in the back so that you are really comfortable by the time you get to the front. When this is completed, let it sit for a while.

Avoid the following. It will not look natural if the lines are too far apart, too straight or start at the bottom. You also don't want the lines too close together, too curved, too wavy or too deep.

When the mountain has dried, we can apply the final touches. Flexrock®

Note the paper maché mountain with the lights in place. Flexrock™ will give the appearance of rock outcroppings. Paint the entire mountain in gray tones.

gives the appearance of rock outcroppings. You may have to search several hobby shops to find it. Cut five or six small pieces from the sheet and trim off most of the backing. Apply glue and randomly pin them to the surface as above. Retrieve the paper maché that you have stored in the refrigerator. Use it to fill in the area around the raw edges of the Flexrock *(bottom of photo)*.

We are finally ready to paint. Color all vertical surfaces, including the Flexrock, Dolphin Gray. Lightly spray random areas and tops of the Flexrock with Moss Green. Sprinkle D56 Grassy Ground Cover over the wet paint. It is important to stop now and let everything dry.

The last step in painting is to highlight the extremities of the rock surfaces. Dip a fan brush in white paint. Remove most of the paint and wipe the brush on paper. "Pull" the brush down the mountain from top to bottom, just touching the tips of the styrofoam. Highlight all of the vertical surfaces in this manner. You will be amazed at the results.

Use several colors and types of stones to create the roads.

Beside the fact that the Romans were great soldiers, they were also experts at building aqueducts, walls, and roads. Our Roman roads are a combination of pet fish-tank or (floral) decorative stone, sand, and D56 Grassy Ground Cover. Use several colors, such as mauve, yellow and pink stone. I mix all of the above ingredients in a coffee can.

This is the time to paint all road surfaces with a thick coating of white glue. Pour the rock mixture over the glue. When this is dry, seal it with a heavy coating of 3M® Super 77™ spray adhesive. Add reindeer moss, palm trees, and flowers. Although winter temperatures can dip to 32 degrees in Bethlehem, it is a rare occurrence. Moderate climate conditions prevail most of the year so flowers are not uncommon. Step back and take a look. Our mountain has reached the sky!

The Desert & The Sea

(3) 1" X 2' X 8" Styrofoam Sheets
Platform dimensions 3' X 8'

The River Jordan journeys 65 miles

south from the Sea of Galilee and terminates just east of Bethlehem in the Dead Sea. The salt content of Dead Sea water approaches 27 percent and will not support life, hence the name. As a comparison, ocean water has a salinity of approximately three percent. So what does any of this have to do with our display? I wanted to have, ancient fishing boats with fishermen hauling in bountiful nets, exploding with fish. So, I took some artistic liberties and moved the Sea of Galilee down from the north and placed it due west of Bethlehem.

Let's start by prying the mountain loose from the styrofoam sheet that we secured it to when we began. Remove the screws and store the mountain in a safe place. Remove the duct tape from the sheet that is taped to the workbench. We will draw the Sea of Galilee onto this sheet. Measure along the leading edge, from left to right, 24 inches and mark it "A". Starting from "A" mark it at 22 inches "B" and 44 inches "C" respectively. Measure from "B" perpendicular, towards the back, 44 inches and mark it "D". Draw a slightly wavy arc from "A" to "D" to "C". Cut along this line to form the sea. With a hot wire or hole saw, re-cut along the same line at a severe angle, to form the beach. Wire-brush the beach so it slopes gently to the sea.

We will need a base for the water, so place the second sheet of 1" X 2' X 8' Styrofoam on the workbench. Paint the bottom of the first sheet with white glue and stick the two sheets together. Screw them with 2" sheetrock screws, inserted on an angle, just as we did when we put the mountain together.

Draw the Sea of Galilee to cover the desired area.

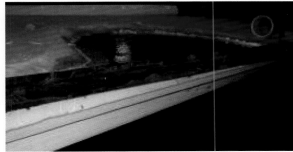

Wire-brush the beach so it slopes gently to the sea. When prepared, add EnviroTex.

Apply water base caulking along the entire beach line making certain that the two sheets are completely sealed. Run a gloved finger over it blending it into the sea. Wipe off any excess.

It's beach time! Apply a thick coat of white glue over the entire beach and extend it one inch into the sea. Spread play or beach sand over the glue and pat it down. Lift the boards vertical to the bench and tap it gently to remove the loose sand. Clean the workbench. Before you continue, make sure the beach is covered with sand. First remove any sand that may have spilled into the sea and then spray the beach with the 3M® Super 77™ adhesive.

And, the Lord said,
"Let there be oceans and seas".

You will need a role of the metal vent tape that is used to seal clothes dryer vent pipes. You'll find it in the plumbing department. Cut off a piece that will extend two inches beyond each end of the sea, about 48". Remove the backing. Start two inches from the opening and align the tape with the bottom of the bottom board. Smooth the tape against the styrofoam, with your finger, across the entire opening and two inches beyond. Cut off a sec-

ond piece of metal vent tape, the same length as the first. Starting at the same point, but this time secure half the width of the tape underneath the bottom sheet all the way across. Fold the remaining half up over the back of the first piece of tape. This will make a firm seal so the EnviroTex Lite® will not seep out. *(See photo above.)*

We have finally arrived at the point where I disclose the secret of how to make the water look absolutely real.

A) Take a tube of caulking and make small wavy lines, some short and some long spaced out over the entire surface of the sea area just as real waves would be. Take a break now and let this dry at least overnight. Two days would even be better. The second part of the "secret" will arrive in stage "B" , after the EnviroTex has been poured and set.

Are there any artists in the audience? Now is your time to shine. Paint the sea dark blue, with a water base paint. I use Glidden®'s "Blazer Blue". While it is still wet, add a one-inch stripe of gloss or semi-gloss white paint along the shoreline. Take a damp sponge and blend the blue into the white. Work it in both directions until the blue gradually fades from very dark into a very light color where the water meets the sand. If you are really coura-

Sometimes you have to take artistic liberties. The Sea of Galilee and Bethlehem are only separated by a cliff. RIGHT: The water and beach look very realistic. Adding the starfish is a nice touch, so are the green shrubs.

geous, lay a thin strip of Kelly Green about two inches out from the beach and blend it in and out in both directions in the same way. The paint will be dry in about one hour. That is the time to mix and pour the EnviroTex Lite.

Mix the EnviroTex Lite according to directions. Pour the mixture from left to right, half way up the sandy beach and let it run into the sea. Distribute it equally with the long side of a tongue depressor until the surface is covered. Let this dry for 24 hours.

Part "B" of the "secret". Look closely into the water where the sand actually disappears. Using a toothpick or a wooden skewer, dip it lightly into the white paint. Mark the water surface along this submerged sand line with thin white lines following the curvature of the sand bar. Some singles, doubles, some triples, but never in a sequence.

The display incorporates the old Little Town of Bethlehem with the new. Add Flicker Bulbs into the display to represent fire since electricity had not been discovered yet.

Put tiny loops like fishhooks on some. If the sea is calm you are finished. If there is a mild breeze blowing, search out some of the lumps in the water and put a small line of white on them. Be consistent as to which side of the wave you add paint. The windier you like it, the more white waves you must create! But, no matter how calm the day, there are always waves along the beach where the water meets the sand!

THE DESERT

To the south of Bethlehem lies an arid waist land, the Judean Desert. In ancient times, Bethlehem was on a major caravan route. If you research the desert long enough, you will discover, as I have, that sand dunes come almost exclusively, in two distinct shapes. One looks like the letter "S" and the other, the letter "C". We are incorporating one of each in this display.

Take two pieces of scrap 2" thick styrofoam and glue them together. Shape this into an elongated "S". Now shape it from top to bottom to form an inverted "V". Wire brush the surface so it is rough, then paint with white glue and cover it with sand. Repeat the procedure with an elongated "C". Place them side by side at the entrance gate of your village.

YOU ARE DONE!

Three different boats from three different villages made the Thames an international port. It's a detail of the picture to the left utilizing the Historic Landmark series buildings of London. The poster in the back shows several London pubs.
- display and photos by Ed Logan

HISTORIC LONDON STANDS ALONE OR CAN BE THE FOCAL POINT IN A LARGER DICKENS' DISPLAY

The Landmark Buildings of London make an impressive historic statement. The skyline is dramatic. **Ed Logan** of Arizona also added some smaller buildings to fill in space, as well as, balance off the extra large size of the Palaces, theatres and other London landmarks.

As a time saver, consider this easy way of creating water. Buy it! Pictured under the striking bridge is the water mat manufactured by LeMax®. Ed

lightly scattered some real plastic snow over the mat for a very effective river setting. It has just enough shine to pick up reflections and show shadows. The addition of three boats adds impact to the open drawbridge. The display sits on top of a large entertainment center.

Most Dickens' collectors - if they have the space - include the Historic buildings into a giant London town. As massive as these buildings are in com-

The historic buildings of London form the major focal points of a larger Dickens' display. Hand-painted oil paintings featuring an English city and countryside were mounted on the wall behind this village featuring most of Dickens' Village.
- displays by Ken & Gloria Hokazono

Many recent buildings have the glass domes or wings as part of the design. This display does a remarkable job in incorporating them into a single springtime display.

parison to the average Dickens' piece, plus the historical significance, these pieces lend themselves to be the central focal district. Thus, **Ken and Gloria Hokazono** *(British Columbia)*, placed them together in the center section of their 30 plus foot display. A large staircase and walls surrounding a multi-level city square unite this section; provides an area for palace guards and townfolks to congregate; and attracts attention because of its openness.

In villages, such as Alpine, North Pole and others where a mountain scene is desired, the elevations become part of the village, as well as the background. For a natural looking terracing of the buildings, use several different widths of styrofoam to build up the levels. They don't have to be much larger than the buildings that will reside on them, plus some extra area for accessories, accents and trees.

Placing the buildings at various angles provides an artistic touch. It also creates a flow which the eye will follow up the mountainside, bringing the viewer into the depths of the display. Look at the buildings. The arcs lead to the back of the display. As a contrast, imagine all the buildings just lined up in a row. The view stops at the front doors. The eye seems to be blocked by the building barrier from going further back into the display.

Allow space between buildings to provide visual relief from a mass of porcelain. Note how the white areas complement the overall look. Add several trees of varying heights between the buildings - ascending the slopes. These groupings also bring the viewer into the display and can highlight a particular building or group of buildings. The mountaintop chalet is framed by the two sets of trees.

Most Alpine buildings have complex and colorful designs, thus place a building with a simpler design and color scheme between them (ochre colored building above) to separate the highly detailed buildings. This village is small compared to the other major villages, but some Dickens' buildings lend themselves to Alpine, too. The Stump Hill Gatehouse and Windsor Castle facade have been included here. Green's Park Nosegays and most smaller buildings with a half timber design could make this village grow assuming Alpine collectors desire a larger village.
- display/Leigh Gieringer/Millie's Hallmark

MOUNTAINS:
A Backdrop or Integral Part of the Display?

Many mountains serve as a village backdrop while others become totally immersed into the display. It depends on the look you are trying to achieve, and the buildings you choose.

Some layouts *require* a mountain setting. Alpine, featured on the previous page, wouldn't be Alpine without a mountain theme. Alpine is also one of those villages where the buildings should be terraced upward - having many levels - to represent various elevations in a mountain scene. The elevations are a distinct part of the display, not just a background. Snow Village has several buildings which lend themselves to a mountainous setting like the ski chalets and rural cabins. New England and North Pole both fit into this category. In fact, any large display is going to have elevations so all the buildings can be seen.

Mountain backdrops aren't really appropriate for some settings. London and New York come to mind. Hills; or concrete, steel and glass canyons are more realistic. Buildings serpentine along long - mostly horizontal - city streets. Some streets will be higher than others so the buildings can be viewed. However, tall backdrops frame and unite the display - providing a finished look.

Appropriate posters with mountains settings *(right and page 58)*, are excellent alternatives for small spaces, but large displays require a custom approach.

BACKGROUND MOUNTAINS

▲ *Styrofoam background mountains are economical and versatile. These were cut from 8' x 2' sections of 1½" styrofoam and placed in front of an uncut piece. The blue protective cover was left intact to represent a blue sky:*

▲ *Shape the edges to give the illusion of greater depth.*

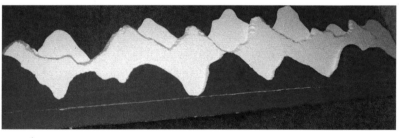

▲ *The peaks and valleys of the second layer are lower and deeper than the one behind it. One inch spacers are attached between layers to create more depth. Purple lights are placed in the gap to provide an evening glow. The third layer is the reverse piece that was cut away from the first layer pictured above. If you look closely, you can pick out the corresponding shapes. If desired, this layer can be kept blue which depicts a late afternoon shadow in a mountain environment.*

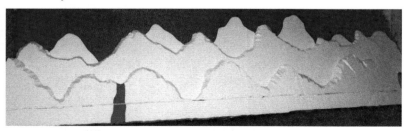

▲ *Or, the backing can be removed leaving a small blue area denoting a waterfall. During the Holidays, North Pole or Dickens' Village is set up. Then the snow melts.*

Living in Colorado, **Nanette Mueller** is inspired by the beautiful mountains around her, and has brought them into her home. She fit several sheets of styrofoam between the top of the kitchen cabinets and the ceiling. Periodically, she changes out the villages and the seasons by replacing the foreground with rolling hills. The frontal range was wrapped in green fabric when the "snow melted" in the springtime.

With spacers in place, fabric is an easier solution, however, different sections can be painted to represent summer or fall and be substituted throughout the year. The benefit is that these buildings can be enjoyed all year.

Having a series of peaks behind the buildings provides more depth to the display which sits above the kitchen cabinets. The blue "sky" makes the mountains stand out. Imagine a purple cast behind the layers to provide a soothing atmosphere when the room lights are dimmed. - displays and photos by Nanette Mueller

The space above the kitchen cabinets provides room for a relatively large display of buildings. Larger accessories can be seen from below. Smaller pieces can be seen if they are close to the edge. The sky and background mountains stay; while the snow "melted" on the frontal range. Change out the front piece to match the season.

GEODESIC FOAM MAKES REALISTIC, BUT LIGHT WEIGHT MOUNTAINS, ROCK OUTCROPPINGS, TUNNEL PORTALS & RETAINING WALLS TO INCORPORATE INTO ANY VILLAGE DISPLAY.

- display and photos by JD Robb

Each section can become a small vignette.

BUILD MODULAR

The previous display technique represents a quick way to develop a setting - applicable for those in a time crunch. It works for all villages. However, developing small sections throughout the year is another time saving solution. Because each section is relatively small, they can be boxed to safely store them, as well as keep them clean. When it becomes time to display them, most of the work is done. Just add the buildings, accessories, trees, etc. Modifications can always be made at any time.

The first step is to form a shape for the mountain with cardboard strips.

Creating realistic mountains is not difficult according to **JD Robb** currently living in Virginia. He perfected this technique while building an awesome display which covered a huge basement in his former mountain-top Colorado home. That display was featured in *Village Display Tips: Series III / Number 3.* JD describes this mountain building process.

This model was used in two seminars: "*Adding Trains to Your Display*" and "*How to Build Very Strong, Light Weight and Realistic Scenery.*" My wife, Pat, and I have a theory that village displays should be: 80% D-56, 15% realism and 5% whimsy. If you build that way, you will capture anyone that views your display. Having been a model railroader for years, the realism segment really appeals to me.

When we build a display, we attempt to make the mountains, trees, rivers, waterfalls, stone walls, etc., as realistic as possible. These features combine with the buildings to form an overall integrated picture. Everything blends as the display comes together.

A very high percentage of collectors put their villages up on a seasonal basis, then take them down after the holiday. I feel that making

Rocks, walls, and portals are attached to the cardboard structure for a realistic setting. Ballast, sand and dirt can be secured with a 50/50 glue/water solution.

scenery realistic, as well as building it strong, durable and light-weight, makes this a valuable display building technique for porcelain village displays. The setting can be easily displayed and packed away.

Years ago, I used *Hydrocal®* to make my mountains, walls, rock faces, etc., but it's much too heavy to be portable and it can be broken.

The system I use now is called *Geodesic Foam®*, originated by **Joel Bragdon** from California. It is a two part resin process that hardens in a very short time, and is almost unbreakable. For example, the model shown is 4 feet long by 2.5 feet wide. I purposefully used those dimensions so the scenery piece would fit through an attic opening for easy storage. The model has a finished mountain, a trestle, two "stone" walls, a beginning mountain, several pine trees, some track and more. It weighs less than eleven pounds. In my seminars, I hold it over my head with one hand.

One type of foam is used for the base, the other for rocks, walls, portals and other detailing. After drying, it is painted.

This process has two different parts; one type of foam is used to form the structure of the mountains, and the second resin is used for detailing. Called Cast Satin™, it is mixed and poured in latex rubber molds. There are various molds to form a variety of rock faces, walls, tunnel portals, etc. Bragdon has at least 30 or 40 different molds that he sells, however one can make their own by buying Liquid Latex Rubber™ - available at model train stores - and painting it over a rock that has interesting features. I have made 20 - 30 over the years. Joel is very helpful and will spend as much time as desired on the telephone about using his process*.

The base I use is an insulation board called "*Tuff-R®*" made by Dow. It is not the blue or pink sheets. I find that hot glue and some paints will eat through them. Tuff R is made of a foam called *Polyisocyurate*. It is cream colored and seems to be impervious to anything I have used to glue or paint it. It also cuts well with a serrated edge knife, like a bread knife. Other manufacturers make a similar product.

I start by gluing cardboard strips into a rough shape of what I want the mountain to look like. Fill several different molds with the resin. After they set, peel the simulated "rocks" away and hot glue them to the cardboard skeleton. Stone walls and tunnel portals are made in the same fashion.
www.bragdonent.com

Allow some flat areas to put track and buildings. Since the structure is hollow, provide openings for the cords to drop through to connect to electrical strips inside the structure. Paint with brush or sponge - dark colors first to create depth.

The last 1/64 of an inch; ie. the painting is the hardest part. It's easy to think that Mother Nature makes chocolate brown mountains and kelly green trees. Not so! Most things in nature are muted or pastel-like in their natural state. Look at pictures for coloring ideas. Most mountains are tones of gray, taupe, ochre or red with dark and light accents.

Ballast, dirt and miscellaneous stuff on the ground is useful. I collect coffee cans of dirt whenever I see some that looks good. I spread it on the layout, and wet it down with a fine mist spray bottle of water. Using an eye dropper, dribble a mixture of 50% water and 50% white glue on all the ground cover. When it dries, it all stays in place**. Add some foliage and other vegetation.

Cost wise, I estimated that I spent about $50.00 building the display model. My thought was to make a "unit" each year and design them so that they fit together to make a village scene. For example, for a New England theme, make a water front module and the following year, make a farm scene to fit next to the water front, etc. That process would make the set up and take down a little easier, as well as, having some hard core realism!

***Placing a similar solution in a spray bottle with a small amount of dish soap to help break up the glue also works. Spray over the entire surface and let dry.*

Bob O'Connor of California uses Geodesic Foam for his displays. It is perfect for water scenes. Blue plexiglass provides a glimpse into the abyss. The boat, skier and shark are motorized to encircle the lighthouse. - display by Bob O'Connor

The coloration in the foreground picks up the hues from the poster backdrop providing a complete setting for this Season's Bay display featured at the Southern Regional Gathering. Molded rocks meet surf. The "Stone" wall is painted plastic.

WATER, WATER...
And, So Many Different Ways To Create It!

Imagine a display without any water in it. It doesn't have to be a large area. Whether a river wanders through Dickens' Village, ocean waves slap against some rugged rocks in a New England display, a rushing stream meanders high in an Alpine setting, or a small, irregular pond breaks up a mass of porcelain buildings in a City park; adding water to a display not only adds interest, but it's fun to create. And, it doesn't have to be difficult.

Sometimes it is not an option. The Tower Bridge of London requires water. How silly would it look if that piece was placed in the middle of other buildings and no indication of water was implied? It's not unusual to have dry river beds in Arizona, but not along the Thames. Or, it could be placed in the background with just the spires showing. That would be a valid solution to not deal with water creation. After all, the buildings in the front can hide the river! That's plausible, and a worthy solution for the new Brooklyn Bridge. But, the Tower Bridge is so striking. It should be a focal point of any Dickens' display.

Some of the lighthouses and other waterfront pieces are set on blue porcelain platforms. That irregular mass of blue represents water and would look ridiculous if the design element was not extended. Again, these pieces could be placed toward the rear of a display, but that eliminates the uniqueness of these

Massive pieces are difficult to place, but they can also be the most interesting. The simple way is to place the building on a sheet of blue plexi-glass, a water mat or any blue surface; or in the rear of the display so only the spires can be seen. However, the setting can be dynamic with a little effect. - display by Leigh Gieringer / Millie's Hallmark

buildings and the fun of putting them into a realistic setting.

In the last two books, there are several ways to assimilate water. It's amazing that there are so many alternatives. Here are several more. Some are focused on types of build-ings - bridges; and those which have become more prevalent in the past couple of years - the water has been designed into the building itself. Then, there are those stock streams. Let's get creative with them, and several other great ideas.

Several of the newer buildings have blue bases representing water. The easy way is to place them on a surface which is intended to be water, but the blue porcelain is above the rest of the water. Water seeks its own level, thus these pieces always look unnatural when they sit on top of another blue surface as above. What can be done with them?

PLACING LARGE BRIDGES INTO A SETTING

The first step is to place the bridge in the location you have chosen. There should be at least two layers of styrofoam under the bridge: a full base level which will get painted and coated, and a partial one which will be become the pedestals to raise the bridge to the desired height above the water. One 1" pieces were used in this display.

This one is influenced by the display on the previous page. To create the pylons, place styrofoam scraps - of the same height - under each tower. With a sharp paring knife or similar, cut the styrofoam following the contours of the towers, or as above, a bit larger. Also, increase the size on the Brooklyn Bridge, since the bases are quite detailed. Add details of choice: etch and paint or small stones. The mirror doubles the effect. - display by Ray Bukovszky

Cut neatly around the tower bases or add some additional girth. *Refer to photos on pages 60 and 62.*

Remove the excess, leaving the styrofoam sections you just cut under the towers. Anchor them with florist pins or low-temp hot glue. Shape the outer stream banks as desired with a knife or hot wire. If you have D56 rock sections - currently retired - you may elect to use them. That's the easiest way to form a realistic river bank. These sections can be painted to brighten the rocks, remove the snow or to match other parts of the display. They are a wonderful addition to any display.

Paint the water in tones of blue with a sponge or sponge brush as described in *The Original Village*

Display Tips book. Dab the color while the paint is still wet so the tones blend. Note where shadows should be . . . under the roads; near the risers - consistent on the left or right depending on your light source, and under any overhangs. Brighten some areas with lighter hues by adding white. Blend the colors unless white caps are desired.

Continue the brick motif of the towers by drawing mortar lines and matching the brick color, or glue small pebbles to the styrofoam under the tower. If a rough water surf is desired, dab some white onto the pebbles or stretch some cotton.

Once the paint has dried, add either EnviroTex Lite® - the two part system, or Woodland Scenic's Realistic Water® *(solution contained in a single bottle).* The former is available at craft stores, the latter at model railroad stores. Follow the directions on the respective bottles. Pour only a very thin layer: no thicker than 1/8". It will set quicker. If desired, more thin layers can be added. Just make certain they set completely between pourings. If it is too thick, it may not set at all. When the "water" has set, add the bridge, and other accessories.

The Brooklyn Bridge could be treated in a similar manner, however, another possibility would be to position it in the background where the base of the towers would not be seen. The spires can become part of a distant skyline.

...tretched pieces of cotton ...present surf and wake.

GETTING BLUE BASES TO LOOK MORE NATURAL

If styrofoam manufacturers knew what an asset the blue covering is to village collectors, they probably would change it. Throughout this book, it is used in so many different ways. The top picture shows several pieces which have the "water" bases sitting on a piece of styrofoam with the blue protective skin untouched. Since water seeks its own level, it is an unnatural look. It doesn't make any sense to hide the edges with rocks or sand, so other solutions have to be found.

The easiest way to camouflage the height difference is to use small pieces of cotton batting. *(photo 2)* The cotton represents the white surf

...r, the piece can be buried beneath the ...aterline. White bathroom caulking was ...sed to make the surf. Clear would also ...ork if a turbulent sea is not desired. ...t looks much more natural then just ...lacing the building on a blue surface ...een at the top.

Position the building on 1/2" thick styrofoam and cut - tightly following the contour of the building foot print.

Remove the building and the styrofoam underneath it. NEXT PICTURE: *Build up with flat pieces of cardboard until the*

gently splashing or pounding against the buildings or the paddlewheels. Stretch the fibers very thin, so you will be able to see the blue "water" through them when they are set on it. Then place them in appropriate spots: near the front of the boat as it cuts the water, the paddlewheel which churns the water and near the rear to represent the wake. Also surround the blue base to give the appearance of waves slapping the timbers.

If that is too easy, or if you want a better look, lower the building into the styrofoam so the water levels match.

EQUALIZING THE LEVELS

Maintaining a consistent water level is the best visual solution. Use half inch thick styrofoam which actually measures 3/8". Put the piece with the blue base in position. With a shape knife, carefully cut around the contour of the building. Remove both the building and the piece of styrofoam beneath the building. It is now too low, but you will have a clean, even cut. Layer small pieces of cardboard until the level of the building lines up with the blue styrofoam covering. At this point, you can go two ways: the simple and the more complex.

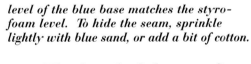

*level of the blue base matches the styro-
foam level. To hide the seam, sprinkle
lightly with blue sand, or add a bit of cotton.*

The Simple Solution: Cover
the seam lines by sprinkling similarly colored blue sand, or sparingly
use the stretched cotton pieces to
represent a splashing surf.

A More Complex Solution:
Tear off a piece of clear Saran Wrap
larger than the base, having the
excess bunch up over the bottom of
the porcelain piece to protect it.
With white kitchen caulking and a
putty knife, create a swirling surf in
a technique similar to frosting a
cake. Allow some of the blue to show
through. Add caulking to the edges
of the Saran Wrap, being careful not
to get it on the building. I've added

The brick pathways in this display are right out of the box, but they can be made to look aged or worn as in the previous picture by using aging compounds. With a piece of cotton, dab a little color - grays for old, brick color for rust, green for weathered copper and so forth. Weathering powders are especially useful for Halloween displays, aging a London scene and weathering water fronts planks and stones.

New   Weathered

some styrofoam rocks for the "surf" to hit against, and a little cotton close to the building. When desired, the building slips out of its hole and is not damaged. Continue the surf to the wharf and around the boats. Instructions for building a wharf can be found in *Volume II*/page 88.

CREATING STREAMS

A down-hill stream, featured on the next page, adds a lot of interest to a display and can lead to a charming waterfront scene.

The base is stacked styrofoam scraps shaped into descending elevations. Two tones of blue sand were sprinkled over the surface which was painted with a glue solution (50% white glue and 50% water). The areas closest to the edges were teal - the darker tone - because the area is shadowed by rock edges. Aqua was placed on the center section since it is in sunlight. The sand was sprinkled in such a manner that there were no hard edges between the colors. A spice bottle with holes can be

The larger CIC waterfront pieces can be merged with New England or Dickens' water themed pieces. Bring the larger buildings to the forefront. Smaller ones recede into the display following the laws of perspective. Concentrate the detail toward the front so the eye focuses on it. The smaller buildings become atmosphere.

used, but there is more control by tapping a spoon to gently spread the sand onto the styrofoam surface.

A small amount of EnviroTex Lite was dripped over the sand and allowed to set. Be careful not to use too much resin, since it will take the sand "downstream" and pool at the lowest elevations. A second coat can be added if a thicker depth, or shinier look is desired. Once dry, a sponge was used to dab white paint to represent a rushing current.

Stream colors were chosen to blend closely with the color of the water under the lighthouse, bird grouping and the Lobster Company to visually merge the pieces with their environment. Blue sand can be added as previously recommended to camouflage the hard edges. The base was not buried here because this is a store display. The lighthouse will be gone when it retires and something new will take its place.

D56 rocky sections formed the drop between the two buildings. They are one of those accessories of which you can't have enough. They are a great addition to any display. The rocks were softened with sand. Real plastic snow accumulated in the crevices.

The edges of the stream look like real rock - because they are real rock: broken pieces of slate. The rock walkway provides a bridge for porcelain residents to wander from Old England to New England.

Although they are different vil-

lages, they are both water oriented and similar is size, thus can easily be placed into one setting. More of a challenge will be to place the Christmas in the City water front buildings in the same display since they are considerably larger in scale.

Place them in the foreground, with the smaller New England or Dickens' Village waterfront pieces behind them. Let natural perspective work for you. It will appear like the smaller New England or Dickens' buildings are in the distance. Accessorize pieces in the foreground, but do less detailing around the smaller pieces in the background.

Thus, the eye will focus more on all the activity around the larger pieces. Another suggestion is to create a body of water between the two villages to separate them.

MORE PIZAZZ FOR THE QUICK & EASY STREAMS

One of the questions I hear most often is how to work with stream pieces. Many collectors have end to end stream sections running through their displays. When they come to the edge of the table, the stream stops abruptly. Many times because they have them flowing in the front of the display, the ends are very obvious. Using these pieces is certainly easier than making streams from scratch, but there are better ways to use these pieces.

You don't need as many stream sections if the stream is broken up with buildings. Use two or three sections mixing the curved with the straight. Place some buildings and trees which will cover the end of the creek sections. On the other side of the buildings, continue the stream, using more or less pieces, then continue with more buildings. Keep the stream curving. Vary the number of sections and type of sections to make the stream look more natural and interesting. The eye will perceive that the stream is flowing behind the buildings. You save some money, since you will not need as many sections. And, you can get more buildings into the display.

Another suggestions is to have the stream enter into a forest of trees. The ends have disappeared, hidden by the branches. Sections can also flow behind an escarpment of rock, enter a tunnel or meander towards the back.

Creek sections all come with patches of snow, which don't fit into a non-winter season. A season's Bay display features the Mountain Creek Waterfall. It has been so well placed and disguised with lichen, foliage and other green material, that it is difficult to believe it is the same piece that is very appropriate in an Alpine setting in January. The light just glistens off the falling water.

Linda Olsen *(Arizona)* built a meandering stream through a Snow Village display. The majority of it was winter, but there is a section of it that showcases non-snow buildings. Pictured on the next page are sections of stream that have been "summerized". Pieces of D56 Lichen - in various colors - were placed over the white patches of snow. Instead of the snow-covered trees that came with the creek, non-snow covered evergreens were substituted. What a great look!

The Mountain Creek Waterfall fits beautifully into this summer setting. Green plants are growing where the snow once existed. The poster backdrop blends perfectly to complete the Season's Bay setting.
- SRG - 2005

ELIMINATE THE SNOW AND STOCK CREEK PIECES LOOK ENTIRELY DIFFERENT.

Streams are easy to create with the stock Mountain Creek stream sections, and they look natural. Because they are modular, they can be configured in a multitude of different ways to fit any village layout. But, they all have snow on them.

Linda Olsen carefully removed the snow from view to use them in a summer scene. She covered the white patches, and merged the shore into the setting with various colors of Department 56 Lichen. Evergreen trees which do not have snow on them were substituted for those that came with the sections. The stream looks very realistic, and it was easy to create. Small boats, rocks, wildlife and other appropriate accessories can be added if more detailing is desired. If not, it is a peaceful addition for any village scene. - display / Millie's Hallmark

This display resulted from the combined efforts of two collectors - each with his own specialty: The water is quarter inch thick silicon which is shaped with a toothpick, and the castle walls are all hand carved and painted, including the terret towers.
- Water by Mike Bretl / Walls by Jerry Fernon

WATER, WATER EVERYWHERE & NOT A DROP TO DRINK

Isn't it truly amazing that there are so many ways to assimilate water in a village display and they all look so real. The water on the previous page was created by **Mike Bretl**. The display was a dual effort with **Jerry Fernon,** both from Florida, who created the walls and cobblestones. The tool he used was his own invention. The special nib fits onto a Department 56 Hot Wire tool. Its function is to keep the width and depth consistent no matter on what surface he is engraving. That is why the grout lines look so even. A toothbrush, with several rows removed, was used to paint the grout lines. Periodic touches of green represents moss growing on the sides of the rocks.

Once Jerry completed the walls and ground surfaces, Mike painted the water area in varying shades of blue. Darker areas give the illusion of depth. The lighter areas are more shallow. The secret is Silicon, applied from a tube with a putty knife. Once again, apply the talents of frosting a cake. Only use in a well ventilated area since it has a strong odor.

Silicon goes on thick - approximately a quarter inch. It takes about 20 minutes to set, but that provides plenty of time to create the churning waves. They are shaped with a toothpick and some patience, but the effect is awesome. Tiny aquarium stones surround the waterline.

Tool can set consistent depth for detailing stones, bricks & drawings

For anyone who has tried to make the mortar lines between brick or stone walls or cobblestone, you know that it is difficult to keep them consistent. Similarly, try to do a stencil, outlines, drawing or lettering by hand. The result is thick and thin lines, or deep and shallow areas. Jerry in the last display solved this problem with his invention, but **John Ehrenreich** from Maryland has a different solution. He uses the hand engraver and attachment made by the *Hot Wire Foam Factory*. The Teddy Bear pattern was transferred to the styrofoam. The actual display can be found on page 34.

A GOOD DISPLAY IS THE COMBINATION OF ALL ELEMENTS. THE BACKGROUND & FOREGROUND WORK TOGETHER AND MERGE FOR A TOTAL EFFECT.

What easier way to add water to your display than to find a suitable background poster where a river or oceanscape is featured. Then, build your display around it. Rose Heidkamp's English countryside display incorporates the water in a very clever way: It appears to be flowing into her display!

The blue and white fences above are made from blue and white plastic cross-stitch canvases. - displays and photos by Rose Heidkamp

It's difficult to see where the background ends and the display begins because the elements are proficiently integrated. The people are in the poster and the swans are in the display. Colors throughout blend. Springtime displays can be so colorful!

BRING THE BACKGROUND INTO THE FOREGROUND

Posters, in the proper scale and subject matter, make dynamic backgrounds for a small village display. Look for ones that are soft or somewhat blurred so they recess into the background. **Rose Heidkamp** from Ohio chose a beautiful river scene meandering through the countryside to add to her Dickens' springtime vignette. The detailing is incredible.

Many collectors would merely place the porcelain pieces in front of the poster, but not Rose. She widened the river - into her scene by coloring the adjoining styrofoam in tones similar to those in the poster. A layer of clear silicon caulking was applied for the sparkling wet look. There is a similar extension on the other side of the display. Seven

swans-a-swimming took advantage of these cozy sanctuaries.

This display is a modification of an earlier display that Rose created several years ago which was featured in *Village Display Tips: Volume II (page 51)*. If you develop a good general layout, it can easily be altered to change the look with a minimal amount of effort. That way the display always looks fresh and interesting.

Extending the water into the display is not the only revamp. Buildings were switched out. They were angled differently. A stone pathway, made of three varieties of blended stone compliments the Season's Bay Fountain. An open-air patio was added to the Tea House, complete with tiny "wrought iron" tables. The patio floor is constructed out of wooden coffee stir sticks aged with a blue wash (watered down paint). The blue fences surrounding it are formed from teal plastic counted cross-stitch canvas. Patterns are easy to create and repeat by counting and cutting away the unwanted squares.

The tables and chairs in the third picture on this page, are beads and jewelry pieces. The crumpets are clay and the patio stones are little plastic tops. Silk flowers become trees, and the "Tea Garden" sign *(page 74)* is the silver-plated D56 Celebration Tray. The detailing is awesome! Posters do make great backgrounds, but so does wallpaper!

This 10" high roll of wallpaper is perfect for an English village backdrop. Obviously, the choice of porcelain buildings should go with the background. Thatched roof buildings without snow would be ideal. Create a smooth transition by extending the roadway into the foreground. Add flowers, trees and other accessories.

SCENIC WALL PAPER CAN ACCENT CURIO CABINET SHELVES, BOOK CASES AND OTHER DISPLAYS

Some wallpaper designs are appropriate for porcelain village backgrounds. Rolls, found at home improvements stores, are 10" high and the pattern repeats, but many shelving units can be adjusted to that height. Measure the length of the shelf and paste the scene on a piece of Foam Core or other thin, but sturdy backing according to the instructions on the package. It can also be applied directly to the wall or cabinet back, but remember: *that is permanent.*

Pictured above is a roll with an English countryside theme, a popular choice for Dickens' collectors

who have some non-snow thatched roofed buildings. The above building is more to show scale, since it looks out of place with a summer background. There is also a pattern which features a French Café suitable for a City background, and others with seaside settings, and more.

The most important thing to consider is the scale of the drawing. Whether the subject is strictly scenery or if it includes some buildings, the wrong scale is detrimental. The emphasis should be on the porcelain buildings. Since they are in the foreground, they should appear larger than those in the poster.

Scenic landscape wall paper follows the room walls providing a background for this "G" Gauge train.

Also pay attention to the colors. Look for patterns which contain the same tones as the houses to be placed in front. As previously stated, if the background photo is soft - colors blurring together - it recesses into the background and brings more attention to the buildings.

The third concern is the transition between background and foreground. Extend the background into the foreground by duplicating, as best you can, the elements in the wall paper. In this case, bring the road, flowers and trees foreword by matching colors and proportions, or place buildings in front to hide the road. Continue to add flowers, trees and other suitable accessories.

NEED ROOM TO DISPLAY? GO UP!

Bud Layman of California designs custom overhead track support systems for "G" Gauge trains out of fine wood to fit any room. As the train travels along the track, it passes in front of a scenic wall paper landscape. A "G" Gauge train is one of the larger scales, thus it can be easily seen from below, but just think of the possibilities.

Imagine a similar track or even a decorative shelve encircling the room. A wall paper scene can serve as the background and porcelain buildings can be artistically positions along an "ON30" or "O" Gauge track. It is one way of enjoying a lot of buildings while not having to use precious living space. After all, when they are in the boxes, no one can appreciate them. This scenario would be especially effective if there is a second story loft and the track or shelf can be seen from above.

AND,
THEN
THERE
ARE REAL
SIMPLE
WAYS TO
ASSIMI-
LATE
WATER:
ROCKS &
CRUMPLED
PAPER

ROCKS,
SCISSORS,
PAPER:
WHAT
MORE DO
YOU NEED?

▲ *Another simple way to create a look of water is through the use of aquarium rocks. Linda Olsen used them in her Snow Village display. Note the placement of the two colors - the darker stones are concentrated in some areas and the lighter stones in other areas, with a soft transition between the two colors created by the rock placement which avoids any hard edges.*

◀ *In a hurry? Styrofoam backing to the rescue again! After it's stripped off the styrofoam, it's intentionally wrinkled, giving it the appearance of moving water. It looks best from a distance, thus a good option for the back of a display. It's cheaper than purchasing blue fabric, comes in long pieces - the size of the styrofoam - which can be cut to desired size or wander through the display. It has a shimmer to it which catches light effectively and is easy to position into place. Put tiny rocks or other natural materials on it to add some realism and appropriate silk flowers along the banks.*

*- display by Ray
& Joan Bukovszky*

6
SEASONAL DISPLAYS
Provide Year Round Atmosphere

It used to be only Christmas, but now, buildings are available for year around enjoyment. Since there aren't too many pieces *yet* for the non-Christmas holidays, small vignettes are the perfect way to showcase the Valentine's Day, Easter, St. Patrick's Day, and the July Fourth Celebration holidays. Enjoyment time is typically two or three weeks before and/or after the occasions.

There are two very good solutions to displaying these vignettes. The first is containers. The hardest part of a container display is to find a suitable one. Look for appropriate containers or props around the holiday you wish to feature. For instance, the obvious ones are heart shaped boxes for Valentine's Day and large pastel Easter baskets and Easter Eggs. They are easy to find during those respective seasons. You may also find some good containers in antique stores, garden centers, import stores or garage sales.

Some less obvious containers are musical instrument cases, hat boxes, wooden produce cases, garden pots and other unique pieces large enough to accommodate one to a few buildings in and/or around them. All the buildings don't have to be contained. The item can be used to simply unite the display - to visually hold it together using form or color. This chapter will concentrate on these special holidays, the next on other types of vignettes.

Valentine's Day boxes set the stage for this early spring display: Add some lights, ribbons with heart motifs, and red flowered silk picks, plus the Valentine's Snow Village pieces. The key is to spend a little time at craft stores prior to the season and see what red, pink and white accents can be added to complete the scene. - display / photo by Edwina Snyder

The other solution is to set aside an area somewhere in the house such as a mantel, window seat or special table just for seasonal displays. As the holiday or season passes, change the entire display to reflect the next holiday; or merely changes the accessories - leaving the buildings intact. Here are several examples.

RECIPE FOR SPRINGTIME DISPLAYS: LIGHTS, SILK FLOWERS, & HOLIDAY INSPIRED ACCENTS

Even the minor holiday collections grow each year. Set aside an area which can feature a small vignette. Build it on a board or in a basket so the base fits into a storage box. As the calendar advances, pack one up and bring out the next, using the same space. When the village gets a bit larger, expand to the space immediately outside the container. Place the new building on coordinating materials, and repeat the coloration. Another alternative, build another similar section which can be

▲ *Look what the Easter Bunny brought?
Feathers are big this year! The white boa
softens the pastel bulbs. The lights also
reflect their colors on the basket. What a
great effect! The basket can be put on a
table, window ledge or even on the floor.
After Easter, the buildings can be returned
to their boxes and the basket placed into a
storage container. - Edwina Snyder*

merged with the existing display, or
create a separate setting nearby, re-
peating the design elements of the
original display.

Sometimes that requires some
planning. For instance, the Valentine's vignette by **Edwina Snyder**,
(Arizona), consists of just three
Valentine's Day buildings *at the
moment*. Next year, when another
piece comes out, adjustments will
have to be made. However, the specialty lights *(or another prop)* might
not be available next year, therefore
it might be prudent to pick up two or
more sets *(or pieces, packages, etc.)*
when they are available so they can
be included in the expansion. Thus,
the displays will look coordinated.

Since holiday specialty merchandise that can be added to these
vignettes varies from year to year,
it's also fun to look for new themed
items to add to or update the scene
for a new look. Bringing out the
same display in future years has its
advantages, too. It's small so it can
reside in a large box during the off
season, and the majority of the work
is done so to reuse it as is definitely
saves time and money; and the holiday atmosphere is still observed.

LATE SPRING: Cover the snow with vines of Foliage to hide the snow patches from sight. Custom bases were designed and built by Bob Herman

DILEMMA: SOME BUILDINGS HAVE SNOW ON THEM. OTHERS DON'T. AND, THAT LOOKS STRANGE IN THE SAME DISPLAY. LET'S FIX IT!

The first Christmas in the City St. Patrick's Day piece has snow on it to match other CIC pieces. That was appropriate since in March in many parts of the Northern Hemisphere, snow is on the ground, and the City is a popular snow trimmed village. However, the following introductions were designed without snow. When a small St. Paddy's display is built, there are three choices. Ignore it. Change it. Or, eliminate the one building that has the snow on it and work with the others.

Let's go with option two. Again, there is a choice. Eliminate the snow on one building, or put snow on the others.

The above picture uses Woodland Scenic's Foliage to hide the snow. It is a stretchy material intended to represent moss, vines or other vegetation and does a good job of covering the snow patches. But, the display will look unnatural if the foliage is applied only to one building with snow. Add a small amount to one or two of the other buildings to balance the treatment. The same treatment can be used to de-winterize any building. The green tones shown are appropriate for spring and summer settings, while the gold, orange and brick tones create a dazzling fall and early winter display.

Foliage comes in little blankets. Stretch it to different densities. Some areas should have more solid coverage. It works well on the stone fences and walkways, hanging from trees and covering rocks - even styrofoam rocks, or rock extensions. Tiny ribbon flowers and those punched out of colored paper can be added to make flowering bushes and vines, but small scaled silk flowers are the easiest way to add color.

To winterizing those buildings without snow, place snow patches on the roofs. It's much easier and provides a cleaner look if ease and time are factors. The patches look natural on the ground, particularly if a platform, linoleum square or other colored surface is used for the building base. Small areas of Real Plastic Snow should be added to select areas as the last remnants of winter's fury, but snow sticks to the patches. It typically washes off with water.

EARLY SPRING: Becken the Snow Gods. Add the little white patches to the roof tops AND to the ground around the pieces. Or, sprinkle small amounts of Real Plastic Snow to create your own patches since most snow has melted.

Materials to add patches of snow

Materials to hide snow patches. Various colors are available.

VALENTINE'S: Madame Alexander Dolls add a nice touch by following the theme. The white, carve styrofoam and the evergreen boughs are great accents. - displays and photos by Debra Blue

RECYCLE THE SPACE

Debra Blue *(Tennessee)* has modified the space over her mantel with the addition of a piece of plywood. The width over-extends by several inches and is held in place with C-Clamps. It is not flush to the wall to allow the cords to be hidden behind the back edge. This complete, she can address her changing display. At Christmas, North Pole is featured. The buildings are switched before Valentine's Day and again for Easter. When Halloween rolls around, the mantel takes on an eerie look. The display elements change so each display takes on a totally different appearance. Seasonal flowers both add color and finishes off the edges. Note the monitor picture also changes with the scene. Debra's Halloween display can be found on page 94 and 95.

EASTER: Reserve a location to showcase your changing holiday displays. Brighten them up with seasonal flowers and other accents available in craft stores. Suitable lights can be found in stores during the respective holiday season.

CHRISTMAS: Mantels are a good height to see all the detail of a display.

Pieces of stone patterned linoleum can unite the Ball Park series buildings and accessories into a pleasant vignette for the baseball enthusiast. Add some spring "lilacs" and fans will be ready for that first pitch.

YOU DON'T HAVE TO LOVE BASEBALL TO ENJOY DISPLAYING THE LEGENDARY BALLPARKS

Many baseball fans consider the first day of the season a holiday, so let's celebrate it. The ball park series' are perfect groupings for small vignettes. However, that doesn't mean that the display is limited to only the four pieces, bleachers and diamond, plus respective accessories. Other buildings can increase the size and impact of the setting. For instance, the Coca Cola Soda Fountain - and accompanying accessory pieces - are logical additions due to its products being sold at many ball parks. Other buildings to consider include the Lowry Apartments. They could also double as a stately office building since storied stadiums are typically located in town centers. Or, perhaps the city officials are working on urban renewal and are trying to modernize the downtown areas. In that case, add the Gardens of Santorini Greek Restaurant. The column motif on this piece compliments the tavern columns. I can just imagine this

To increase the size of this mini-display, other buildings such as the Coca-Cola building can be added. Several accessories including the Pretzel Concession, the Pretzel Cart, Luigi's Gelato Treats, and the Midtown Newsstand are appropriate.

building located on a hillside behind the Pretzel concession stand. As an alternative, add several others to form "Restaurant Row". Or, the bleachers could be partially hidden behind the trees. Raise them up and cut some of the D56 red brick vinyl to indicate an extended stadium wall. Replicate some of the detailing from the facade to tie it in.

A subway station could be included. Use the retired version if it is accessible, or create some stairs leading down to an implied subway train. The bus or train station would be effective additions. Add the hos-

pital for injured players. With all the cars in the D56 line, a parking lot can also be included.

If this will be a cultural center, too, add the Radio City Music Hall, Ed Sullivan Theater, or one of the art museums. This mini-display is growing. You can probably think of several more buildings to add to a realistic mid-sized display.

Another thought is to build more refreshment and souvenir stands. Make team pennants, fold small pieces of fabric to represent T-shirts, dress some small Teddy Bears in team colors, create some mini-baseball caps, baseballs and bats. They can be formed out of clay, painted and hung on the back and side walls of the stands.

Miniature food - hot dogs, beer bottles, soda cans, apples, etc. can be added. Use your computer to make team posters. Tiny versions can usually be found on team web pages. They are big enough to download on glossy paper. Cut and frame with balsa or basswood. Use them for your own personal use, but don't reproduce them in quantity or you could run into copywrite problems.

Of course, you can limit the vignette to just the baseball grouping of your favorite team, or collect them all for rec room, home bar or office book shelves. They will also fit nicely on top of a TV, which is what **Tom and Teresa Brader** from Louisiana did.

They had one building and several accessory pieces which they wanted to feature, but it was important to them to have an infield, too.

Their display rests on a 1½" thick styrofoam base enabling them to form intersecting streets. Wrigley Field was placed in the center, at an angle to face the intersection. A knife and straight edge was used to cut the bricks, then painted slate gray to blend with the base of the stadium. To obtain the rough texture on the nearby streets, Tom used the knife blade to scratch away the top surface unevenly resulting in a bumpy appearance. Streets were painted in tones of brown. On one corner, a fire hydrant was fashioned out of clay. On the other, a four inch dowel - painted black - was used to represent a globe street light. The white ball is clay, but a wood circle could be used as well. They are attached with hot glue.

A hole was made through the styrofoam to accommodate the light cord. A cord channel runs underneath towards one side so it lies flat and allows easy access to the switch. Then, it drops to the back.

The diamond behind the stadium is quite exact. It has brown base paths and an on-deck circle. The infield lines and batter's box was painted white. A small piece of styrofoam - about 3/4" high - was cut into a oval, shaped, glued down and painted to represent the pitcher's mound. Under the pitcher is a white pitching rubber. Who's on first? Third's empty, and second is an illusion. The bases are wood squares. The field was painted in tones of green and sprinkled with green turf for a more realistic appearance.

Stadium fences are 4"x2½" cedar slats. A saw blade created vertical lines every ½" to represent wooden boards. A few knotholes were added with an awl.

Recent additions include the Souvenir Shop, Refreshment Stand and more people. The display comes out on Opening Day and stays on the TV until the World Series is over, even if the Cubs aren't participating.

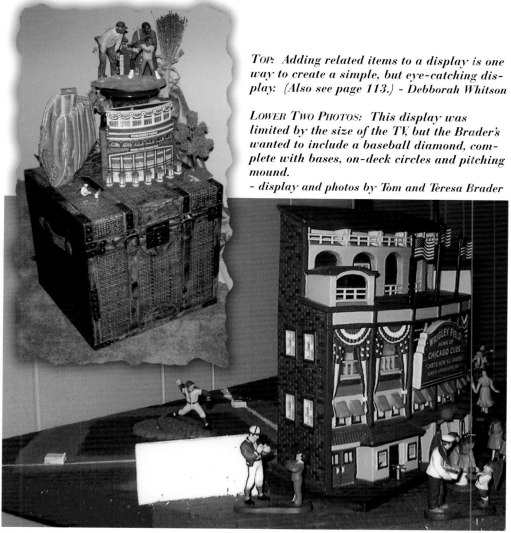

TOP: *Adding related items to a display is one way to create a simple, but eye-catching display. (Also see page 113.) - Debborah Whitson*

LOWER TWO PHOTOS: *This display was limited by the size of the TV, but the Brader's wanted to include a baseball diamond, complete with bases, on-deck circles and pitching mound.*
- display and photos by Tom and Teresa Brader

This display can be put almost anywhere in the room. The builder has the choice to have a frontal focus, or create it so it is interesting from every vantage point. Inspired by a display featured in the Fall, 2004 *Celebrations* magazine, **Ray and Joan Bukovszky** created their own adaptation. The display uses a 30" sonnet tube - a hollow construction form used with concrete. Building contractors or suppliers should be able to obtain them.

Drill a hold on the bottom large enough for the plug end of an electrical strip to pass through. If desired, line the interior with a soft fabric, not that it is seen, but so you can store the display boxes inside the container. About six inches below the top, attach a round plywood circle with brackets. It will have to be cut down to fit within the tube. Prior to attachment, drilled a hole in this circle, too, to drop the cord through it. Rest the electrical strip on this shelf. Or, anchor it so it will not flip. It is easier to plug and unplug when it is assessable.

Select some fabric, suitable to the display such as the burlap used here. Neutral and solid colors don't distract from the display. Determine the needed yardage to wrap around the cylinder shape. Staples from a staple gun hold up better than hot glue or duct tape to attach.

Rest a 30" round plywood circle on the top. However, to get at the electrical strip, Ray cut a small area away, just large enough to get his hands inside to reach all the outlets in case he wants to switch or add buildings, lighted accessories or street lamps; or if one of the above goes bad.

Cut styrofoam in a circle to fit over the 30" round plywood. Carve and paint the edges to simulate rocks or later cover it with appropriate garland. Build your display depending how it will sit in the room. In this display, the cemetery lifts out to reach the electrical strip.

This size display seems to hold about four medium sized buildings without over crowding. The Bukovszky's used the Hallow's Eve buildings - a small sub-series of Dickens' Village. However, the Victorian Christmas building sub-series also consist of four buildings. Other suggestions include creating a small water scene for New England using a lighthouse and a wharf, or a lighthouse, cliff and rocks; or develop a little townsquare for Alpine. Any favorite building set can be featured in this type of display. The choice of buildings and garland wrap is unlimited to the creator's imagination.

To make it a walk around display, build up the center with trees or styrofoam rocks and angle the

buildings so they back to the center elements.

Another thought is to get a total of three tubes, cutting two into progressively shorter heights. Dress the bases in identical fabric and garland and build a larger display on the trio. If that isn't big enough, get several more all circling the tallest one, but vary the height so the tubes don't look like stair steps. Separate them further with large evergreen trees or other items related to the subject. *There's built in storage!*

HERE'S THAT FIREPLACE AGAIN!

We've seen **Debra Blue's** fireplace displays earlier in this chapter. She expanded the display area to cover the hearth and floor around it. The rest of her Halloween is on other tables. Fabric and orange lights add to the atmosphere. The edges of the styrofoam - carved with a hot wire - were painted black to follow the Halloween theme. Straw - great for fall scenes - covers the horizontal areas where the buildings reside.

- display and photo by Debra Blue

The display on the next couple of pages is a club effort both in concept and in construction, although **Mike Sanders** was responsible for the base box and background construction and fabulous animation.

A couple of pieces from the SV Halloween were added to All Hallows' Eve and sit on the mantelpiece - the same mantel that held Valentine's, Easter and North Pole displays at other times of the year. The fabric background with the flying bats and witches, hides the fireplace opening, and ties the two sections together.

Joint project by members of Southwest Villagers, Phoenix, AZ

SEVERAL HEADS ARE BETTER THAN ONE!

With a little brainstorming, numerous ideas can be triggered by other ideas. And, thus the concept evolved from a simple Halloween setting to whirl pools, sunken ships and treasure chests. The theme, "Alcatrastle" was a combination of Alcatraz Island and Dracula's Castle. It was an entry into the *Golden Gate Gathering* in San Francisco held in the fall of 2003. *The moral: if you aren't able to come up with ideas, discuss it with other collectors. Then, try to figure out a way to construct it!*

Orange lights were placed between the curved painted sky and the black San Francisco skyline - both shaped out of sheets of thin plywood and bolted together to hold the curve. They sit on a wooden base which contains the mechanics and electrical strips. There were three Department 56 pieces. The Pirate Ship was placed on a turn table to make it look like it was caught in a whirlpool in front of the lighthouse, and Dracula's Castle sits on another island in "The Bay". The LeMax Pirate Ship which moves up and down, as well as makes audio sounds, "sailed" the channel. Select D56 accessory pieces animated the display. Several LeMax pieces were also added. A green crypt was weathered to blend more with the castle. The buoys were also aged. Blue Saran Wrap was gathered, wrapped, anchored and capped with white paint to represent a rough sea. The dark rocks extended under the water where another complete scene exists. It was the top winner in more than one category:

Literally; think inside the box. A scene doesn't have to only be above ground. It can be extended below ground: subways, mines, basements, or under the water line. The front section of the base box that contained the electrical, was cordoned off with pieces of styrofoam, shaped and colored to look like rocks which were continuations of the rocks above the waterline. Sand and shells form the sea bottom. A treasure chest and sunken boat were obtained from a fish store. Additional "jewels" were acquired from craft stores and "swimming" children's plastic toy fish were fitted with firm wires. When all the above were in position, a solution of white glue and water was sprayed over the entire scene to hold everything in place. (See Footnote page 57.) Blue Saran Wrap was placed behind the plexiglass window. All rocks were sponge painted black with brown and gray highlights.

Skeleton lights don't have to stand vertically: They are very effective in a prone position in fields, grave yards, caves or under the water.

Little porcelain buildings make excellent decorating items that can be enjoyed throughout the year. Used in combination with interesting antiques and art objects, hat boxes, pottery and so forth, select those buildings whose coloration and/or themes coordinates with your room tones and styling. Try it with your church, lighthouse, or identical themed pieces. - displays by Debborah Whitson

VIGNETTES & SMALL DISPLAYS
Little Space / Large Punch

*W*hat's the difference between a vignette and a small display? The number of pieces contained in the setting, but many argue that a vignette can be comprised of numerous buildings. It is a snapshot focusing on a certain theme. It tells a story or merely expresses the creative visions of the developer. For the most part, Season's Bay can be classified as a vignette, since the entire village is small; or, select some buildings to fit a designated area.

That is the reason why many collector's love it. They have all the pieces, they can set up a display and it will be complete. Like anything else, it can change - if the desire is there. Other pieces can successfully be added. Some of the non-snow New England buildings are very attractive in the background. Multiple cottages can be "built", after all, vacationers need a place to stay and to have identical rental units is not out of the question. But, don't just line them up in a row. Vary the angles and distances between them for a more interesting visual impact and natural setting.

Due to its relaxing resort atmosphere and a more accurate scale of buildings to accessories, it is *Sandi Moore's* favorite village, and she keeps it up throughout the year - in different variations.

A styrofoam base is covered in moss green fleece. Each season, she removes all of the pieces, vacuums away loose snow and

WINTER, SPRING, SUMMER, FALL: THE SEASON CHANGES EVERY THREE MONTHS FOR ALL.
(At least in this Season's Bay Display.)

- display and photos by Sandi Moore

dust, and rebuilds the display. The light cords are pul-led through the fleece, thus are buried, but accessible. This display is positioned on her fireplace mantel. Since the mantel can't accommodate all the buildings at once, they are rotated in and out which also keeps the display interesting and fresh.

To clean the pieces, she dusts them twice a month with a make-up brush and uses a can of pressurized air intended for cleaning

A light dusting of snow indicates Santa's on his way. It also allows other landscape features to remain visible. In March, the snow is vacuumed up, (an easier task when there is less of

computers. Remove small accessories first. Don't get too close to any delicate areas with the air.

Winter arrives in mid-December, and leaves again in March. In June, the change to summer is quick and simple. Trees or buildings do not have to be altered. Just the accessories are switched. Autumn changes are the most fun and colorful. Then the snow flies again.

it); buildings, trees and accessories are swapped and the off-season pieces are placed in small display cases until their season returns. The interactive involvement adds to village enjoyment and swap time is not a dreaded event.

The worst part is packing and unpacking the pieces. To avoid that, Sandi puts the off-season pieces - by season - in three small and separate display cases in her office so they, too can be enjoyed all year.

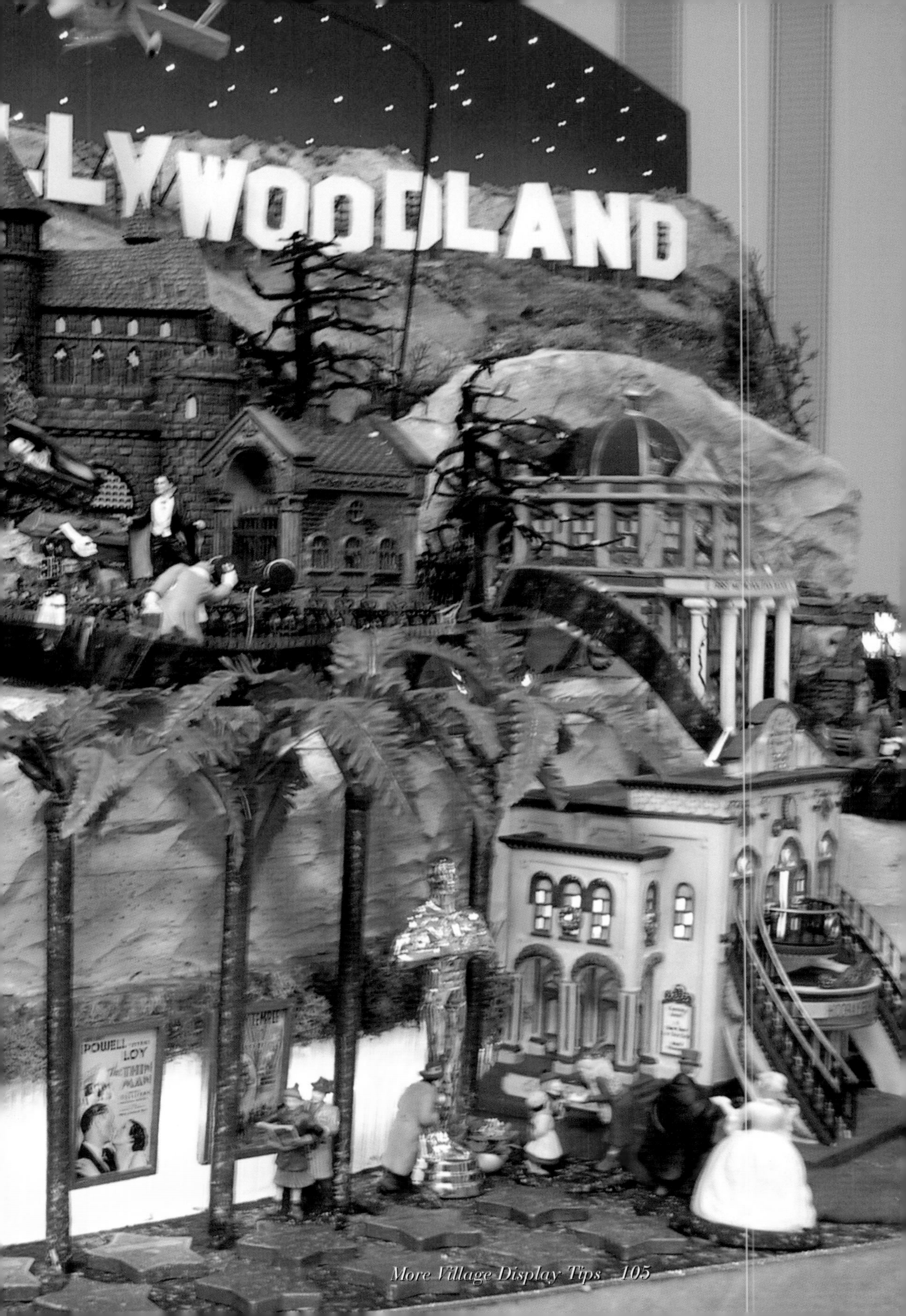
LYWOODLAND
POWELL
LOY
THIN
MAN

TRIBUTE TO HOLLYWOOD, CIRCA 1930'S

The South-west Villagers Collector's Club entry to the *California Gold Gathering* - 2004 portrayed a Hollywood theme. In the 1930's, the sign over the Hollywood Hills actually read: **Hollywoodland.**

In the "Earthquake" scene, it would have been sacrilegious to break a perfectly good building, thus, luckily; the bank building withstood the jolt of the major shock. But around it are remnants of others which suffered major damage - piles of aged clay bricks, stone treasures intended for fish tanks, broken pieces of wood and other debris to lend some authenticity to the setting. Of coarse, the city behind the bank is burning. Flicker bulbs, Saran Wrap and a small fan make it very realistic.

LOWER LEFT:
The red carpet is out for the latest Hollywood Premiere. Wedding cake columns were painted metallic gold and small potted plants complete the formal setting.

TOP RIGHT:
In the 1930s, the sign read Hollywoodland. Wood scaffolding holds up each letter. A 1930's airplane circles the mountainside.

MIDDLE RIGHT:
Framed movie posters which all date back to the late 1930's line the walkway.

BOTTOM RIGHT:
The club version of the Hollywood Walk of Fame. Each member who worked on the display has their own walk of fame "star". Animation created by J. Michael Sanders

The Dracula set consists of the D56 animated pieces. The background "rocks" were etched and colored to match the castle. The LeMax Crypt was weathered. Actually, it was the same one from the Alcatrastle display done the year before. There is an eerie green light inside. Each movie set features a camera to shoot the action.

Each letter of the word Hollywoodland was cut out by hand out of Foam Core board. It is difficult to see the back, but the scaffolding which holds the letters up is accurate - done in thin pieces of balsawood. A 1930's era plane circles the "Hollywood Hills".

The three movies that are featured date back to the thirties as well: *Earthquake, Dracula* and *Gone With The Wind*. There is a lot of animation and special effects throughout the three movie sets. All of them have cameras on set. In the Earthquake movie set, the bank building sways from side to side. Bits

and pieces of rumble lay next to the lucky bank building which miraculously was spared. However, it was set deeper into the ground, while it moved from left to right. The city is in flames behind the building. A combination of flicker bulbs, small sheets of Saran Wrap wave to make the fire more realistic. Wind flow is courtesy of a small fan built into the display.

The Dracula set was fairly simple. A LeMax crypt was aged to blend better with the castle. Some Department 56 animated pieces provide additional animation.

Filming just began at Tara.

Scarlet, Rhett and cast act for the camera which sits on a child's toy. The arm was removed and attached to a motor so it arced from side to side recording the scene. Landscape consisted of turf, small rocks, and sand applied as described in previous chapters. The curved styrofoam backdrop was painted.

Scarlet and Rhett and crew played their parts well. The camera caught it all as it moved across the set. The yellow arm of the camera is actually part of a child's erector set. The camera was made out of cardboard.

Gala festivities are taking place at the theater as the Who's Who of the Hollywood elite gather at the Premiere. Movie posters, downloaded from the internet, line the wall along the star-studded Walk of Fame. Along the sidewalk are the "stars" responsible for working on the display. All club members took a name of a famous 1930s movie star.

The palm trees are all hand made. Leaves were stripped from several silk flowers. The trunks are masking tape, rolled tightly around a metal wire, then painted brown. The Oscar statue was found at a discount store. Accessories which looked appropriate were added to the walkway.

The antique can of movie film is authentic, dating back to the thirties. Film was strung throughout the display to tie all the different elements together. The display is about 60"x48". The frame is wood and the elevations are made of styrofoam. It received a First Place recognition.

IF YOU HAVE A COLLECTION OF ALL THE SAME TYPE OF BUILDINGS, HOW CAN THEY BE DISPLAYED?

Restaurants can be lined up above the cabinets or in an out-of-the-way spot in a kitchen. Schools, lighthouses, churches or - fill in the blanks - can be individually displayed in bookshelves, plant shelves or as table centerpieces into small vignettes. But, what if you want to display them all together? Here is an idea supplied by **Ray and Joan Bukovszky** of Arizona. They set several Dickens' Village Churches on a round table and separated them with Pencil Pines. It is a simple solution, but very effective and appealing. Furthermore, it works!

- display by Ray and Joan Bukovszky

Because each scene is part of a circle instead of simply lined up, the viewer only sees two or three other churches at a time. The trees, green flat picks and accessories visually separate those in sight. Thus, the eye can concentrate on and appreciate each individual church. The center greenery, ornaments and candles provides a background, help hide the electrical cords and adds some festive, seasonal color.

THE NCC CLUB HOUSE SITE OF RED HAT SOCIETY GATHERING. YOU WON'T WANT TO MISS IT!

A hat box became the base of this vignette. The red feather boa truly makes it pop! ***Pat Murray***, of Arizona used the Red Hat Society theme with the NCC clubhouse, and 'announced' the Spring Fling on the sign that is included as part of another village accessory. The Red Hat ladies came from Hallmark®. They are part of a bubble-light (nightlight). The figure separates easily from the light and are a perfect size to coordinate a village setting.

The flower gardens were made in a Department 56 Gathering Make 'N Take. The yellow tones compliment the Club House and add contrasting color to the display. Red Hat Society colors of red and purple were used throughout the rest of the display. Pat took the 'auto with tree', painted it purple, and exchanged the tree for the baseball cap from the D56 Christmas "Collector" Ornament. Whatever 'red & purple' items that she could find were added. *Pick a theme. Find a container. Gather related items. Get busy!*

- display by Alexander Whitson

DRESS UP A THEME WITH RELATED ITEMS

Big into cars as most teenager boys are, **Alexander Whitson** has learned a unique display building flair from his mother, **Debborah**. Select one or more favorite buildings, and gather items that relate to them. Wheel hubs, tool boxes, and actual car parts are visually held together by a bundled, heavy-duty extension cord. This is a very creative approach to showcasing any porcelain or ceramic building or sets of similarly themed pieces. These displays can be set on floors, steps, staircases landings, or table tops as decorator items. As stated on the last page, select a building or two, and start gathering associated items. It's so simple, and so effective. Little

or no styrofoam. No carving. No engraving. No painting. Creativity plus. They can be ultra striking. And, each display is uniquely yours!

On the facing page is a New England theme sitting on a high shelf in the Whitson family's entryway. Another section of this display is featured on the spread including page 1. Woven grapevines *(large photo)* hold the display together. Fish netting, shells, and weathered twigs combine to tie the boats, lighthouses and other buildings and accessories as a unit. Select porcelain accessories complete the scene which can be left up throughout the year and/or periodically changed.

Let your creative juices flow!

- *display by Debborah Whitson*

CONTRIBUTORS 8

*A*ppreciation is extended to the following collectors who submitted ideas and/or were invited to contribute to More Village Display Tips. *These ideas will offer many new creative options for other collectors to follow and enhance their enjoyment, as well as their displays. Special thank you's are given to Peter George, publisher of the* Greenbook to Department 56 Villages *for writing the Forward, and to Millie's Hallmark, Phoenix, Arizona for allowing their displays to be included and providing several buildings for illustration.*

Debra Blue
Tennessee
Halloween & Seasonal
ii, 81, 86-87, 94-95

Tom & Teresa Brader
Louisiana
Wrigley Stadium
90-91

Mike Bretl
Florida
Water
72

Ray & Joan Bukovszky
Arizona
Vignettes
62, 80, 83, 92-93, 110

Bernie Dvorak & Team
Maryland
Little Town of Bethlehem
ii, 2, 36-47

John & Pat Ehrenreich
Maryland
Vignettes
34, 73

Jerry Fernon
Florida
Engraved Walls
72

Rose Heidkamp
Ohio
English Countryside/Alpine
6, 59, 74-76

Bob Herman
Arizona
Lighting, Platforms
8, 32-33, 84-85

Ken & Gloria Hokazono
British Columbia
Historic London
37, 49

Bud Layman
California
Backdrops
78

Ed Logan
Arizona
Historic London
ii, 37, 48, backcover

Sandi Moore
California
Elfland/Season's Bay
2, 9-17, 101-103

Nanette Mueller
Colorado
Mountains
51-53

Patricia Murray
Arizona
Vignettes
35, 111

Bob O'Connor
California
Mountains/Water
58

Linda Olsen
Arizona/Millie's Hallmark
Snow Village Designer
Water
i, ii, 7, 59, 71, 79

J.D. Robb
Virginia
Geodesic Foam Mountains
2, 51, 54-57, backcover

Leigh Gieringer has been creating village displays since 1988. She is a graduate of the University of Wisconsin with a degree in Fine Art. She has compiled, written and published the Village Display Tips books, Village Display Updates and produced the Village Scaping Videos and DVDs: resources for village collectors to help them enhance their village displays. She was a feature writer for The Village Chronicle, and currently for Village D'Lights Magazine; has given seminars at Village Gatherings, store and club events, as well as designed and developed retail store and collector home displays.

J. Michael Sanders & Southwest Villagers Collector's Club
Arizona
Animation/Club Displays
3, 81, 96-99, 101, 104-109, backcover

Southern Regional
Florida
Rocks, Water
51, 58, 70

Edwina Snyder
Arizona
Seasonal Vignettes
81-83

Alexander Whitson
Arizona
Decor Vignette
112

Debborah Whitson
Arizona
Decor Vignettes
vi, 1, 91, 100-101, 113